THE DIVINE HOME

THE DIVINE HOME

Living with Spiritual Objects

BY PETER VITALE

Text by Alejandro Saralegui

Clarkson Potter/Publishers

New York

All rights reserved.
Published in the United States by Clarkson Potter/Publishers, an imprint of the Crown Publishing
Group, a division of Random House, Inc., New York.
www.crownpublishing.com
www.clarksonpotter.com

CLARKSON POTTER is a trademark and POTTER with colophon is a registered trademark of
Random House, Inc.

Library of Congress Cataloging-in-Publication Data

Vitale, Peter.
    The divine home : living with spiritual objects / by Peter Vitale ; text by Alejandro Saralegui—
1st ed.
        p. cm.
    Includes index.
    1. Interior decoration—Psychological aspects. I. Saralegui, Alejandro. II. Title
    NK2113.V58 2008
    747—dc22
                                2008011863

ISBN 978-0-307-40521-0

Printed in China

All photographs by Peter Vitale; those appearing on the jacket and pages 2, 18, 54, 57, 58–59, 60,
156, 159, 160–61, 214, 217, and 218 are courtesy of *Veranda* magazine.

Design by Skolkin + Chickey, Santa Fe, New Mexico

10   9   8   7   6   5   4   3   2   1

First Edition

JACKET (FRONT): The blue-painted gown of a large nineteenth-century Mexican Virgin that originally lay in a
casket complements the decoratively painted walls of the bedroom in the 1807 hacienda belonging to
Marcia Brown in Atotonilco, a small village outside of San Miguel de Allende, Mexico.

PAGE 2: Red-pigmented lime paint coats the walls of Marcia Brown's entrance, creating a dramatic backdrop
to a collection of saddles and other riding gear surrounding a large cross that has lost its Christ figure.

PAGE 4: In the collection of Peter Vitale and Harry Greiner, a pair of nineteenth-century French candelabra
flank an Italian figure of the Christ child from the same period. Silver ex-votos of different sizes add more
brilliance to the composition.

PAGE 5: A marble nineteenth-century Burmese Buddha from the collection of John Gough.

PAGE 8: In the richly decorated home of Marie Carty, a Mexican figure of San Santiago sits astride his horse.

For all those seeking truth, harmony, and love in this universe

CONTENTS

FOREWORD

RELIGIOUS ART AND DESIGN SPRING from the search for an integrated perception of external, visible reality and internal invisible sensation. Therefore, religious art cannot imitate nature but must strive to abstract or idealize it to find a balancing point in man and nature's essentially chaotic relationship. In short, it attempts to bring order to that most disorderly situation: life.

Peter Vitale has amply observed every form of life and every form of religious expression in art and design through his worldwide explorations as a photo-chronicler of culture and lifestyle.

For a number of years I had the privilege to be his friend and collaborator on many features for *Architectural Digest* as well as on several of my own books edited by Jacqueline Kennedy Onassis, who so admired the keen observations of his photography.

He and I were once together in the jungle of Nepal at dawn witnessing a violent and blood-splattered ceremony to appease the local female goddess by beheading male animals (finishing with a temporarily splendid water

buffalo, whose head ended up at the feet of the statue of the goddess). That was religious art at home in its most primal form. I have been with him to photograph a serene Buddha in the otherworldly beauty of a water garden on a Chinese mountainside, and we traveled to Texas and Mexico to photograph not-serene-at-all santos-packed villas—opposite poles of the meetings of religion and art.

In 1978 I was in Venice with Peter Vitale documenting Peggy Guggenheim's (still private) palazzo-cum-shrine to twentieth-century art, where secular painting and sculpture took on the role of a reconciling force that integrates outward perception and inward sensation—two long suits in Peggy Guggenheim's pack of cards.

For my book *Tiffany Taste*, Peter photographed the message-filled dining room of the Hawaiian king's Iolani Palace, where a portrait of Napoleon III hangs opposite the king's thronelike dining chair like the venerated icon of a saint, or of God himself.

We photographed the private sitting room of the German empress Frederick Victoria at Schloss Friedrichshof, where images of her family—her mother, Queen Victoria; her brother, Edward VII; and her husband, Frederick III—were clearly the saints of this intimate family chapel.

In *The Divine Home,* Peter Vitale takes us on a magical tour of richly diverse interiors, where religious art and design from a multitude of cultures stand out in their beauty and intrigue by their capacity to provoke sensations beyond what the eye can see.

Of course, as was the case with our past adventures in documenting the proud possessors of the sacred, the iconic, the fetishistic, or the simply venerated, there is always much more going on than meets the eye.

Long attuned by experience to the complexities of the unspoken messages of interiors, Peter Vitale leads us in his photographs in *The Divine Home* to recognize the purposiveness of religious art as it animates its surroundings. Wisely, he makes no attempt to editorialize. He shows calmly and clearly the situation in which the symbols of religion have been placed, where they can awaken whatever sensations they may as we observe them in all their beauty, artfulness, or idiosyncrasy, their purposes (and often their very nature as religious objects) redefined by their collectors.

Each image in *The Divine Home* depicts not just things in artful arrangement but also a complex state of mind embracing both the visible and invisible.

John Loring
February 6, 2008

INTRODUCTION

Explaining birth, death, night, and day has been the province of religion from the very first days of human history, and artists have also struggled with the issue of our existence. As civilizations spread across the globe, art forms developed and artists began creating symbols that reflected their beliefs. To this day, we don't know why the prehistoric peoples of Lascaux and other early communities drew bison and outlines of hands on the walls of caves. Perhaps it was an effort at depicting their environs or a way of giving importance to their lives on earth. The art that the homeowners in this book have collected for their personal enjoyment was created with these very thoughts in mind.

OPPOSITE: Various sculptures of Buddha from the collection of John Gough. TOP LEFT: An eighteenth-century gilt Burmese seated Buddha. TOP RIGHT: A nineteenth-century alabaster Buddha head from Mandalay. BOTTOM RIGHT: An eighteenth-century Thai Buddha in wood. BOTTOM LEFT: A rare Laotian nineteenth-century Buddha head.

Examining the undeniable beauty of crucifixes, Buddhas, santos, masks, paintings, and all other manner of devotional objects amassed by the grand acquisitors on these pages takes the spiritual artworks to another level. Not only do the pieces practically tell a story on their own but also the collectors have stories about what attracted them to these objects. It might have been the peaceful face of a nineteenth-century Peruvian santo or the gilded wooden rays of sunshine that emanate from a halo or the arresting color of a ceremonial Thai jug that originally interested the buyers of these pieces.

The collectors here have accumulated objects that represent many religions from across the world. Some are no longer practiced and their artifacts are barely understood. Some continue to offer people hope and solace. In both cases, among the art that these religions produced are works of great beauty enjoyed by believers and non-believers alike. That these objects have survived decades, if not centuries, of use and neglect speaks to their craftsmanship and the importance bestowed upon them by the original creators. Funereal objects, which were often buried with the deceased, were meant to long outlast the corpse, as in the case of pharaonic treasures discovered in Egyptian pyramids. Later, the tombstones of Greeks and Romans were sculpted as reminders of the fallen. Following in the steps of Judaism, the rise of Christianity added the concept of celebrating life on earth as worthy of artistic attention. Personages in both the Old and New Testaments, whether real or imagined, were looked upon for divine intervention and inspiration. Not only were images of the crucified Christ created but also the iconography of a host of heavenly angels and saints was developed to show people how to live with one another in peace.

All these traditions and many others are the basis for devotional art that is collected today. From the dreidel that Jewish children spin during Hanukkah, reminding them of the ups and downs in life, to bi-discs, the ancient jade grave markers of our Neolithic ancestors in China, these objects are collected today for their meaning as well as their artistic merit. The owners of these artworks live with their collections in a variety of ways that wasn't imagined by the original creators. Some live in spare simplicity, amid a few carefully chosen, essential pieces that contribute to the sense that their homes are a decompression chamber from their multitasking, twenty-first-century lives. Others live with an Aladdin's cave worth of treasures.

The homeowners presented here find pride in their homes and their far-reaching art collections. More important, though, they all find comfort in the environments that they have created, seeing them as places of refuge and relaxation. Examining how centuries of art create their magic in a deeply personal manner is the goal of this book. Within, we see that santos and reliquaries are enjoyed by their current owners for their intriguing forms and histories. Liberated from behind the railing on an altar, they now hold pride of place poised on a sideboard or turned into a lamp.

Naturally, for many collectors, an attraction to homes with historic character and an appreciation of antique devotional objects go hand-in-hand. Homes requiring extensive renovations and/or restorations are not the exception with these collectors who value the history of their possessions. Some of the Santa Fe homes featured here have been brought back to life with thick plaster walls and wooden vigas holding up the roofs in a tradition that was started by John Gaw Meem, a leading

A window ledge in Ford Ruthling's home holds an array of objects ranging from Chinese blue-and-white vases to a pair of angels on Corinthian capitals surrounding an eighteenth-century Mexican santo.

Santa Fe architect, who renovated and built homes in the local vernacular. A Houston couple demonstrated a love for their roaring twenties house with a slow and historically accurate renovation.

Many of the people featured here also take pleasure in mixing religious art with other important collections. One New Mexico family has their fair share of santos and angels, but the wall space goes to a growing gallery of top-notch Southwestern paintings from the twentieth century. A photographer in Manhattan lives with that most precious of commodities: space. Her double-height living room is grounded by a very select group of sculptures ranging from ornate Baroque to Minimal. In Dallas, a jeweler who in a former life sold contemporary art has blended her passion for art from the sixties and seventies with devotional objects full of meaning.

All of these people have opened their homes to share the beauty of their collections. Living with religious art may seem odd to many, but to these aficionados it is a natural part of their lives. Religion and the artifacts it has inspired continue to bring comfort to us. Whether seeking a traditional spirituality or not, these collectors have amassed collections of divine style for their personal delight.

A nineteenth-century French *resplendor* highlights an ancient Egyptian stone bird, creating a harmonious image at the home of Peter Vitale and Harry Greiner.

An extremely varied collection of crosses is mounted above a seventeenth-century Jacobean settle with antique-textile cushions in Dianne Cash's home.

LAYERS OF OPULENCE

LIVING HISTORY

An artist's lifetime of collecting art

SANTA FE, NEW MEXICO

"AT FIRST SIGHT IT LOOKS AS THOUGH I'm a raving Roman Catholic," comments Santa Fe, New Mexico, artist Ford Ruthling. "But I was actually raised Lutheran! I'm not attracted to these objects for their religious purposes [as much] as I am to their outward beauty and craftsmanship." Indeed, Ruthling's house is a repository for all manner of Catholic art from the past five centuries. The collecting bug bit him early on. As a teenager during the Depression in nearby Tesuque, he used to buy bogards, a southwestern Native American wrist ornament, with money he had saved up. Now his collection of more than fifty examples has increased in value considerably.

As of late, Ruthling's collecting bent has turned toward reliquaries, the containers or shrines in which holy relics of saints and Christ are believed to be kept. He says he doesn't collect the artwork thinking he has a piece of Christ's crown of thorns or the bone fragment from a saint. Instead, the object itself is the prize. Ruthling is especially drawn to quillwork reliquaries made by nuns and monks in medieval Europe. The art of quilling, also known as filigree or scrollwork, was a highly valued talent then, and considered equal to, and an acceptable substitute for, praying. Simply wrapping a dyed or gilded piece of paper around a quill or needle creates a scroll, which the artist then affixes to a decorative background. Some examples of quillwork are so intricate that they resemble three-dimensional damask. One of Ruthling's reliquaries contains ten pieces of bone, from several specific saints, held in place by pearl bands and surrounded by elaborate quillwork. At first glance, another reliquary looks as if it were filled with accessories for a dollhouse, but actually the miniatures in the frame represent the Instruments of the Passion. In the Gospels, these objects are described as tools in Christ's death, such as the dice the Roman soldiers used to cast lots for Christ's robes or the sword He was stabbed with. The reliquary's glittering background is made of crushed amethysts glued to a black paper support.

PREVIOUS SPREAD: Ford Ruthling's living room features a circa 1890 crucifix on the far wall by New Mexican artist José Benito Ortega. On either side are retablos by José Rafael Aragón from the same period. Above the sofa is a Mexican Colonial painting of Jesus at the post. Originally from a church altar, the gilded dove above the painting represents the Holy Spirit.

OPPOSITE:

ABOVE LEFT: Detail of a seventeenth-century scrollwork reliquary from Assisi, Italy. The medallions are wax and on the reverse represent the Agnus Dei, or Lamb of God. They are believed to have special healing powers and may not be bought or sold.

ABOVE RIGHT: Various examples from Ruthling's collection of more than seventy-five reliquaries create a rich display. On the Sheraton side table are a pair of gilded altar decorations.

BELOW RIGHT: The background of this circa 1700 Italian reliquary is crushed amethyst glued to black paper. The objects themselves are all related to the Crucifixion of Christ.

BELOW LEFT: The two standing Christos are by José Rafael Aragón and represent a bloodied risen Christ. Ruthling made the pillows on the sofa by attaching vintage vests to fabric and suede cushions.

ABOVE LEFT: An antique Peruvian silver repoussé retablo depicts a scene with the Sacred Heart in the middle. To the left on the shelf below is a santo of Saint Sebastian, who was killed by arrows. The santo head on the right has an elaborate gold halo more typically seen on members of the Holy Family. The gilded snakelike santo is contemporary. Photographs of friends and family are framed in antique tin frames.

ABOVE RIGHT: Several processional pieces from Mexico and Peru. The largest one has a retablo of the Virgin Mary at its center.

BELOW RIGHT: The bones, supposedly from various saints and holy figures, on this seventeenth-century French reliquary are held in place by pearls and are carefully labeled. Painted scrollwork with gilded edges fills the background.

BELOW LEFT: A French sixteenth-century Virgin and child found in Beaune decorated with tempera paint and gilding. The orb and lilies are not original to the piece.

The secular architecture and culture of New Mexico is also extremely important to Ruthling. In 1977 four of his paintings of New Mexican Pueblo pottery were selected to be the images on U.S. postage stamps. Ruthling's antique Pueblo pots, which he has been collecting for about forty-five years, appear throughout his Territorial-style house, a three-acre property just blocks from the historic Santa Fe Plaza. "The style of this house is marked by a more formal look than Pueblo architecture," Ruthling explains. First developed during the gold rush of 1849, the Territorial style is marked by East Coast stylistic details such as brick coping along the top edge of the walls, shutters, and square columns. "The other predominant architectural style here is pueblo, with its thick adobe walls, vigas or beams sticking out, and little decorative steps called Mabel's ears." The Mabel in this case is Mabel Dodge Luhan, a wealthy Easterner who moved to Taos in 1919 and became enchanted with the native culture and people, eventually divorcing her husband and marrying a Native American named Tony Luhan.

With its extensive garden, including Ruthling's own version of a garden folly, the house is a popular stop on garden tours. Rimmed with blue stucco walls and rambling roses, the covered garden space serves as a refuge where Ruthling and his partner, Robert Mason, relax and watch the hummingbirds feed. They have adorned it with a multicultural mix: a large Indian goat sculpture, green Thai rabbits, and additional antique Mexican pieces. Flanking the goat are a pair of *palmadores*, sometimes called *florales*, antique Mexican tin representations of the floral arrangements that were once used to decorate altars.

Although Ruthling has difficulty selecting a favorite object, he cites his collection of santos, carved and painted images of saints, as particularly dear. "I have quite a few from all over, but I especially love the New Mexican santos, because of their rarity." It turns out that the rarity is due to Archbishop Jean-Baptiste Lamy, a Frenchman immortalized in Willa Cather's *Death Comes for the Archbishop*. Lamy objected to the cruel and obscene nature of the santos, often depicted mutilated or dying, and urged his parishioners to destroy them. Older santos, such as those made by José Rafael Aragón in the 1880s, are sought out by collectors today. A crucifix by Aragón in Ruthling's living room represents a gory, bloodstained Christ on the cross wearing a skirt or kilt instead of the normal loincloth. According to Ruthling, "The New Mexicans of the period were embarrassed by Christ's nakedness on the cross and showed him with a more demure cover-up." An eighteenth-century Mexican santo depicting Saint Peter is draped with a silver wine-tasting cup from Ruthling's membership in La Confrérie des Chevaliers du Tastevin, the French wine-tasting society. "Oh, he's just become a place to hang things!" Ruthling exclaims. "I've resigned four times from that club."

A wall of retablos and reliquaries. The three pieces down the center are seventeenth-century Italian reliquaries with an architectural churchlike design. To the right are traveling bibles and money pouches.

OUTSIDER EXPRESSIONS

Discovering and appreciating the inner lives of artists

EVERY PIECE TELLS A STORY HERE. And generally speaking, each one tells a big story. Eugene Frank is a collector of different sorts of spiritual art. His collections vary from Outsider art to African works to Judaica. As a psychoanalyst, Frank seems drawn to the human tale of the artists, and he bases his collecting on the effect their pieces have on him. A few years ago, he decamped from Georgetown, from a private practice he held for many years, to Santa Fe, where he is now writing a how-to book for present and potential psychotherapy patients. "There are many parallels between Georgetown and Santa Fe," Frank says, explaining his choice of a new home. "Both have a great mix of cultures, which results in a very interesting lifestyle that I find attractive."

Twenty-eight-foot-high wood-beam ceilings give this art-crowded house a gallery-like feel. Two intimate seating areas with furniture, mostly seventeenth- and eighteenth-century pieces that this Francophile collected in France, leave plenty of room for art. The striking surrealist artwork above the fireplace, framed by two tall windows, is a favorite of Frank's. "It is an intensely unnerving image. The idealized woman's face comes from a Medici tomb in Florence, and the man's arm is extremely powerful. The artist drew it in ink and charcoal on corrugated cardboard, which looks almost x-ray-like. You cannot help but feel something about this piece," he says. Another surrealist piece dominates a wall of art hung in the manner of a Victorian parlor. The hyperrealistic painting of a man and a tractor in a marble quarry makes a statement about the impact of society on our lives and the way the coarseness of civilization is wiping away the softer side of life.

Two crucifixes serve as great examples of Frank's Outsider art collection and his generosity toward artists. Frank discovered the artist who created the larger of the two by chance, outside of Taos, New Mexico. He had been exploring a jumbled wreck of a building with a

PREVIOUS SPREAD:

A rare Pennsylvania Dutch country cupboard with flaking blue paint and a brass Early American chandelier stand out amid the devotional and Outsider art in the dining area. On the far wall a seventeenth-century hand-carved pine mirror hangs from a larger mirror in a seventeenth-century gilt frame that was cut up to give a surrealistic impression.

OPPOSITE:

ABOVE LEFT: A Guatemalan polychrome and gilt crucifix purchased at the Chimayo shrine in New Mexico. Flanking it is a pair of old Native American pots from Santa Fe.

ABOVE RIGHT: An array of Outsider art in the stairway. Framed in a blue altar, the painting of a very large pear is by Carol Anthony. Frank has attached his own objects to it. A favorite painting of Frank's, with cartoonish images of the American dream, hangs above the stairs.

BELOW RIGHT: Frank met artist Candice Johnson in Paris, where he purchased nine of her portraits. He later framed them in concrete, iron, and barbed wire. A 1923 tax stamp on the mystery novel advertisement to the left confirms the authenticity of this rare poster.

BELOW LEFT: This large crucifix contrasts with much of the Outsider art in the stairwell.

friend when a stranger came out and asked if the visitors liked his art and wanted to see more. Frank and his companion accepted the invitation, and the artist, Jake Harewell, drew them back into the building, where he showed them a collection of artwork that bore a slight resemblance to the work of Christo. Apparently the artist had collected skins discarded by a nearby drum factory and used them to wrap objects, giving the objects a spooky, otherworldly effect. "My crucifix is made of two old railroad ties, and the head is from a mannequin," Frank explains. "I loved this intensely tormented piece, and bought it right there. It was the first piece Harewell had ever sold. I went on to introduce him to other collectors and dealers, and he became a sensation in the Outsider art world." Frank is impressed by the artists' need to express themselves and let their inner demons out. "Outsider artists pour their heart and soul into their art, and we gain by understanding their problems without directly experiencing them."

Another Outsider artist Frank introduced to the art world, Phillip Estrada, created the other crucifix. Estrada had been living in Brisbee, Arizona, a small mining town, when Frank came upon his artwork. Estrada's grand-mother worked in a baby doll factory and would bring home the irregular dolls, which Estrada would then mount on crosses. "I wanted these artists to teach me how to feel in other ways," Frank says, "and his artwork is very effective. I convinced him to make more and come to Washington for an exhibition. He turned up with seventy-five crosses for the show, and William Paley bought six."

The Candice Johnson piece adjacent to the dining area is made up of nine portraits. Frank's partner at the time created the concrete, iron, and barbed-wire frame for it. "Candice lives in Paris, and we became friends over the years. She always paints the same portrait, over and over again. She is probably some sort of schizophrenic, and like so many other Outsider artists, she had a need to create in order to survive and externalize her demons."

At the other end of the emotional spectrum are artworks that just make Frank smile and laugh. Hanging in the stairway, for example, is a painting of a blond woman with a house floating in the air behind her amid a naïve landscape. "It was painted by a very large man," Frank comments. "There is no perspective to it; it's very child-like, but there is an affectionate aspect. You just have to enjoy this piece and see the silliness and humor."

The voluminous living room provides much-needed wall space for this eclectic collection of art. Drum skins, a mannequin head, and railroad ties make up Jake Harewell's cross on the top half of the wall. Below it a hyper-realist painting by Bruno Schmelz represents the encroachment of the civilized world.

An exploration of African art and culture

Eugene Frank bought his first piece of African art at age eighteen as a young man in Paris, where he now has a second home, and has continued buying pieces that speak to him for completely different reasons. While traveling with friends through Europe, he happened upon a Chiwara antelope headdress in Paris that set off the collecting bug in him. "I didn't even have the money at the time, and the dealer let me take it, and I wired her the money when I got back home! I felt the power of these pieces and have since learned about the history of the objects and the cultures of the people that made them." Combining the physical characteristics of an antelope and a human being, the Chiwara headdress holds pride of place in the ritual dance for a good harvest of Mali's Bamana people.

While in Europe, Frank noticed that African artworks were much more integrated into the European lifestyle than in New York, where he grew up. "The Germans, French, Dutch, and Belgians brought these objects back home with them from their colonies in Africa," Frank explains. "Over time the objects became part of the European scene and were eventually the inspiration for Cubism." Looking at Frank's early-twentieth-century West African Yoruba sculpture of a man with a torso that narrows to nothing, triangulated legs, and circles for hands, it's obvious that this geometry is where Picasso and Braque got their inspiration. The Yoruba, whose culture goes back at least to the fourth century B.C., have influenced not only Western art but also the Santería religion

in Cuba and Puerto Rico. Inspired by what he has seen, Frank now feels it's natural to live with his extensive collection of African art all around him.

There is a kinship between these African art objects and the Outsider art Frank collects and displays in Santa Fe; both stem from the artists' need to cope with a world they don't understand. The spirit of the makers and the codified rules that went into creating these powerful objects also attract Frank. "*Fetish* comes from a Portuguese word meaning an object endowed with power," Frank says. "The object that has been created as a fetish has a power that you can feel and practically smell when you hold [it]." Frank owns a lion figure that was originally found at the entrance to a village; its history serves

OPPOSITE:

ABOVE LEFT: This male lion figure is actually a tree that had fallen and was carved right where it fell. A real tortoise shell hangs from the hand-forged steel chain.

ABOVE RIGHT: A very rare pounded-copper mask from the Dinga tribe, who live between Angola and the Congo.

BELOW RIGHT: A trio of power figures from different African tribes. The figure to the right is a nineteenth-century Nkisi, or nail fetish, from Nigeria.

BELOW LEFT: An eighteenth-century Benin culture bronze python that, along with a fabric body, may have been placed on top of a royal palace. The artifact rests on a piece of Kuba cloth woven with a traditional geometric pattern.

as a good example of the belief in totemic power. Apparently a tree had fallen and someone carved the trunk into a figure of a lion with whiskers and placed a metal scrap on the head, indicating a mane, with the idea that the lion would protect the village. A hand-forged iron chain and the carved carapace of a turtle known to close itself up entirely complete the trifecta of protection for

OPPOSITE:

In the foreground are a pair of bronze eighteenth-century leopards from Benin. On the center right of the wall, the white round mask is a very rare téké-tsaayi mask from the Congo; it was used in a dance as an affirmation formalizing the social structure of the village.

FOLLOWING SPREAD:

LEFT PAGE: In the dining room, African masks and power figures are assembled above the French nineteenth-century credenza.

RIGHT PAGE, ABOVE LEFT: Frank displays this nineteenth-century turquoise-studded, silver Mexican kaddish prayer book in a Plexiglas box with a photocopy of a prayer for the dead on the back.

RIGHT PAGE, ABOVE RIGHT: A wrought-iron menorah, prayer shawls, and prayer book.

RIGHT PAGE, BELOW RIGHT: A triptych of images that Frank assembled: The subject of the top photograph is anonymous, but it reminds Frank of his grandfather and of Marcel Proust, a literary favorite; the two works below are contemporary but deal closely with the Holocaust.

RIGHT PAGE, BELOW LEFT: A Passover-offering plate juxtaposed with pictures of Frank's grandparents, whose preparation of the Passover meal was their offering of thanks to God for being here and alive.

the village. Frank describes the lion figure as an apotropaic object, one that averts evil.

Frank's grouping of Judaica has a completely different, intensely personal meaning for him. His mother gave him her father's little velvet bag with a star of David on it that he used to take to the synagogue for prayer. She framed it and put her father's name in Hebrew on it. A little doll figure is from Frank's Bar Mitzvah cake. "My maternal grandfather was extraordinarily dear to me," Frank says. "He was the one who took me to museums as a child and taught me so much about music." A nineteenth-century Mexican Kaddish, a book of prayers for the dead, in silver with turquoise inlays, is framed in Plexiglas. And below that are three art objects mounted together as a triptych of Frank's own making. The top image is a photograph of a man who reminds Frank both of his grandfather and of Marcel Proust, one of Frank's literary heroes. The middle piece is by an artist who uses actual passport photos of people who perished during the Holocaust to make little memorials to them. On the bottom piece, unintelligible words stamped in metal, reminiscent of the writings Holocaust prisoners carved into their cells, make up the third little artwork. On the floor sits an African stool with a votive candle, which Frank lights in memory of a deceased partner. "It is so easy to take life for granted," he says, "These are reminders of the sacrifices that people have made for us and how fortunate we are."

S. Cecilia V. y Martir.

EMPIRE STYLE

*International art and antiques from the Spanish conquest
at home in a one-hundred-acre hacienda*

NOGALES, ARIZONA

Some people collect with a geographic interest, some define their collections stylistically, and yet others choose a historical framework to guide their voracious collecting. Eddie Holler and Sam Saunders fall into the last group: their collection of religious art follows the Spanish Conquest throughout the Americas and even includes art from Spain's rule over Indonesia and the Philippines. From Columbus's discovery of America in 1492 to the end of the Spanish-American War in 1898, which marked the end of the Spanish Empire, Catholic art was at the forefront of Hispanic culture. Holler and Saunders's most important pieces come from Latin America, especially Argentina, Bolivia, Chile, Guatemala, Mexico, and Peru.

Holler started collecting in 1972, as a hobby, and then with Saunders opened a gallery about ten years later. The by-appointment-only gallery, featuring about thirty-three rooms full of Colonial, Baroque, and Colonial Revival antiques, is located on their one-hundred-acre hacienda, a privately owned estate comprising several structures, in Nogales, Arizona. The main house, which is about forty years old, was built by Holler's grandfather, who had a produce-importing business that is still in his family. Living with objects that might be sold from time to time hasn't been much of a problem for the men from a decorating standpoint since they can always replenish from one of the old produce warehouses they use as a storage area for their excess collections.

Holler's grandfather played a large role in Eddie's upbringing and influenced his interest in art with a spiritual theme. "As a child, my grandfather used to take me to Guadalajara to bars that were two hundred to three hundred years old. While he was with his friends, I would

PREVIOUS SPREAD:

ABOVE LEFT: A Mexican eighteenth-century santo, most probably of Saint Helena.

ABOVE RIGHT: An eighteenth-century easel or bookrest, called an atil, featuring an image of the Virgin of Guadalupe. The Mexican painted leather crown in the foreground is from the early years of the Spanish Conquest.

BELOW RIGHT: A large School of Cuzco eighteenth-century painting of Saint Michael in a later frame. In the foreground is a statue of Saint Santiago riding horseback. The unidentified eighteenth-century santo in the corner is from Lima, Peru.

BELOW LEFT: A nineteenth-century retablo of Saint Cecilia, patron saint of musicians, playing the piano.

OPPOSITE:

ABOVE LEFT: A gilded arrangement of Mexican Baroque spiral candlesticks in front of an eighteenth-century private altar from a hacienda in Bolivia. The figure inside the altar is San Raphael.

ABOVE RIGHT: In the courtyard, a Mexican eighteenth-century granite angel from Puebla stands on a Ionic column.

BELOW RIGHT: Holler mounted these mutilated figures of Christ on stone orbs, which stand on top of an eighteenth-century Peruvian inlaid wood secretary. Behind them is a seventeenth-century gilded Mexican frame, which now holds a mirror.

BELOW LEFT: A 1700s Filipino Christ child and pedestal. Both His solid gold gown and gem-encrusted crown are original to the piece.

wander about and visit the cathedral and the local palace; little by little, I developed an appreciation for it."

From these frequent trips to Mexico Holler also absorbed an eye for symmetry. "On my walks I just noticed that everything in Mexico was symmetrical, and I liked the sense of calmness that pairs of objects or classical buildings impart." This isn't to say that everything is a perfect match in their home. As long as there are two similar candlesticks or the altarpiece has columns on the left and the right, he's okay. Holler also points out that since pairs are harder to find, it just makes the search that much more difficult, and therefore more fun for him. In one of the gallery spaces, a hoard of matched gilded objects is carefully displayed on an attractive walnut table. The background is a large mid-eighteenth-century gilt altarpiece, protecting a figure of San Rafael, of a type that was used in private homes. This fantastic piece, which comes from a hacienda high in the Bolivian Andes, is flanked by a pair of modern obelisks, two pairs of eighteenth-century Mexican Baroque spiral candlesticks, and a pair of gilded capitals supporting silver orbs.

The figures of the crucified Christ that Holler mounted on thin silver-plated crosses sprouting from stone spheres tell an intriguing story. For the most part, objects in the Holler-Saunders collection are in a remarkable state of conservation, but these little sculptures of Christ have lost their limbs and, in many cases, even their heads. As Holler explains, this is due not simply to age but to a nineteenth-century practice wherein teenage girls would pray for marriage. When the requested match did not materialize, they would chop off a sculpture's arm or a leg until a marriage came to fruition. "I guess," Holler jokes, "that those without heads were the victims of spinsters!"

OPPOSITE:

ABOVE LEFT: A detail from a very large painting of the Virgin Ampona, so called because of her bell-shaped dress, that was found in an eighteenth-century Mexican hacienda.

ABOVE RIGHT: A gilt-wood traveling niche protecting a Virgin Mary. Niches like this one—which even has handles—were taken from home to home by their owners.

BELOW RIGHT: A primitive retablo of the Holy Family enthroned in an agave.

BELOW LEFT: This nineteenth-century crucifix from Michoacan, Mexico, was made for personal use.

LAVISH EXCESS

Early married life in Italy jump-starts a rich collection displayed in Victorian style

SANTA BARBARA, CALIFORNIA

"I've never taken a picture of this apartment that doesn't look like a junk heap!" claims Santa Barbara resident Marie Carty. Admittedly, this jewel box of an apartment is crammed to the hilt, but the sheer quantity of objects doesn't preclude their quality. The simple rooms with arched entrances are the perfect foil to Carty's Victorian salon–style treatment of paintings and objects. Not only are the walls covered from floor to ceiling, but every tabletop holds its fair share of bibelots, from santos to silverware.

Accumulating artworks was never a passion for Carty, until she moved to Italy. "I started collecting when my husband and I moved to Florence in 1958," she notes. At the time, she became what the Italians called a *commissionare*, taking tourists antiques shopping through Florence, and little by little she developed an appreciation for the pieces her clients were purchasing. When she returned to the United States she became a personal property appraiser. "That is when I really became hooked," Carty adds. "I had to go to all the antiques shows, auctions, and galleries to learn about the values of these objects that I was appraising. Then I had the misfortune of a great antiques dealer opening his shop right next to my office, and that was the end of any self-control!"

While there might not be one particular piece that stands out in the living room, the assemblage of objects there is astounding. Everywhere one's eye lands, there is something to focus on. One wall holds four panels of Joseph Dufour's *Views of Paris*, from 1810, originally from a suite of wallpaper that once covered a whole salon. Dufour was a leader in the French wallpaper industry; in the early nineteenth century, the technique became popular as a manufactured way—albeit by hand—of decorating a room. The panels are half-covered by an Italian marquetry chest of drawers and compete for attention with the pair of large Spanish niches above the French daybed. Remarkable in its own right, each gilt niche holds an eighteenth-century Peruvian angel in its center; one contains two Austrian musicians and the other a pair

PREVIOUS SPREAD:

The richly patterned living room is dominated by a pair of Spanish niches with gilded frames above a French daybed. These display frames each have an eighteenth-century Peruvian angel mounted inside.

OPPOSITE:

ABOVE LEFT: A highly animated Mexican santo of San Santiago, with his sword raised ready to conquer Mexico for the Spaniards.

ABOVE RIGHT: In this home devotional, depicting the Stations of the Cross, the back panel rotates so that all of the Stations can be viewed.

BELOW RIGHT: A Virgin of the Immaculate Conception statue. Carty draped the pearl and coral necklace over her shoulders.

BELOW LEFT: An eighteenth-century Portuguese painted and gilded cabinet holds a collection of silver milagros, or ex-votos. A pair of pre-Columbian Zacatecas figures flanks the cabinet. The silver chalice and patens on the right side of the table are a rarity in that they match.

The creamy background doesn't compete with the abundant treasures in this room. Above the camelback sofa are a pair of eighteenth-century falcon hunt pendant pictures that are possibly Italian. The glass case to the left holds Carty's collection of ivories. To the left of the coral chair is a large eighteenth-century Mexican statue of Saint Michael.

ABOVE LEFT: This gilded santo is remarkable for its removable head, which allows one to move it in any direction.

ABOVE RIGHT: Antique Austrian musicians.

BELOW RIGHT: A madonna with a silver crown and elaborately painted dress. To the right is a silver processional staff with bells all around it.

BELOW LEFT: A pair of eighteenth-century Italian reliquaries.

of eighteenth-century Italian reliquary figures. The two arrangements are Carty's own altarlike design. A bit overwhelming on their own, taken together with the other artifacts they simply blend into the background.

The apartment gains grandeur from the richness of its decorations and from Carty's skilled hand for composition. Even the rather plain bathroom door is decorated. Above it a painted Peruvian shelf adds glamour. And nailed to the door itself are several small painted retablos, the oil paintings of the Holy Family on metal or wood that have been used for centuries in home altars throughout Latin America as objects of veneration. These retablos depict the flight into Egypt, the Holy Family in contemporary Spanish Colonial garb, the patron saint of prisoners with manacles, and the patron saint of silence holding a monstrance and a palm branch. A more sculptural set piece is made up from a pair of blue and gold painted corbels on either side of an eighteenth-century silver gilt altar surmounted by a particularly fine Mexican Saint Santiago, sword raised, astride a galloping horse.

"I describe myself as a 'collapsed' Catholic! But that doesn't stop me from buying or appreciating all of these beautiful objects," Carty quips. Everything seems to be presented in multiples. The glass curio case on the living room wall, for example, she describes as "my nonsense case all full of ivories of varying degrees of good—some good, some not so good, and some very good." It is this sense of inclusion, and the fact that she just likes the objects for themselves, that makes Carty's home a place of discovery and amazement.

RESTORATIVE HOME

Building a chapel to exhibit antique textiles and give thanks

SANTA FE, NEW MEXICO

THE TREASURES THAT FILL Dianne Cash's Santa Fe home represent her strong love of art and history. Her travels, especially in Spain and Morocco, provided much inspiration. She describes her house as belonging to a wanderer from Spain who appreciated Mexican and Native American arts. Having studied religion and art, Cash feels it is impossible to separate the two. "I don't think you can study a religion without seeing the art," she says. "I have an appreciation of why it was made." And although she isn't Catholic, she does find herself drawn to objects with Catholic imagery. "Mainly," she notes, "I have bought art because I love it."

Cash's Pueblo Revival house was designed in 1947 by celebrated Santa Fe architect John Gaw Meem for John Crosby, the founder of the Santa Fe Opera. Cash added her own surprising element to the house in 1998: the private chapel, a fusion of several she saw during her travels in northern New Mexico. "There was a time when many houses in the area, particularly those of the wealthy, had their own chapels," she explains. Having battled cancer, she found herself making a pilgrimage to El Santuario de Chimayo, a small shrine just north of Santa Fe that attracts thousands of worshippers during Holy Week every year. "I had broken my back and was going in a full body cast, but I soon realized that my problems paled in comparison to those of others. That was when I decided to build my chapel in thanks to my good fortune overcoming cancer and surviving my injuries," she says. "The construction phase was most helpful because it kept me from thinking about my injuries."

Although not consecrated, Cash's Pueblo Revival chapel was blessed by a local priest on Christmas Day, her birthday. It remains an area for quiet contemplation and an ideal spot to display her extensive collection of liturgical vestments. "These garments are works of art in their own right," Cash notes. "I have a real respect for

A pieced-together mantel of Mexican cantero stone is one of many highlights in this baronial living room. In the foreground is a seventeenth-century Italian chair with vintage velvet upholstery. Cushions made from antique textiles rest on the seventeenth-century Jacobean settle. The early-1800s studded leather trunk is from Morocco. A brilliant array of silver *resplendors*, which originally crowned saint figures, arches over the entrance to the hall. Beyond is a collection of crosses from different centuries.

the people who made these objects with love and dedica-tion." The altar area is a careful composition of textiles and other items centered on an antique South American cross under a Peruvian *resplendor*, a type of sculptural halo. On the altar, an eighteenth-century French chasu-ble, a sleeveless priest's garment, lies over an elaborately embroidered early-1800s textile. On either side of the altar, Italian Renaissance walnut chairs sit below late-seventeenth-century Spanish chasubles hanging on eighteenth-century banners. Mounted in floating Lucite frames, other priests' garments fill the chapel with color and texture. Eastern European pews from Bulgaria, Hungary, and Romania, with colorful floral decorations on the front, line the chapel as if waiting for mass to start. "Now I use the chapel as a place of reflection and meditation," Cash explains.

Elsewhere in the house, Cash's other collections, especially her outstanding furniture, demand equal attention. A large carved canopy bed frame hung with panels of embroidered antique fabric sets the tone for the master bedroom. Gold floral embroidery brightens a late-eighteenth-century textile on a console covered with gold crowns and *resplendors*. With a barley twist–decorated Jacobean chair and a piece of architectural salvage used as a low table, the intimate seating area con-tinues the Spanish Colonial theme. Santos from Mexico

An 1800s Spanish Baroque angel with a period gown. Pieces like this were most probably used in Nativity scenes.

and the Philippines standing on the table remind Cash of modern art. "Looking at them, I'm thinking of Gia-cometti's people walking. They're just friends on a table."

The book-lined living room features a pair of set-tees: an eighteenth-century English tapestry-covered one, and a leather-upholstered American version with a vibrant seventeenth-century Spanish textile. The side table holds several devotional items, including a circa-1750 monstrance, an elaborate gold altarpiece used to display the consecrated holy eucharist in Catholic churches during the mass. The mantelpiece around the simple adobe fireplace was created using two antique Mexican columns and a mantel top. In the front hall, above a seventeenth-century Jacobean settle with a dis-tinctive high back and a seat concealing a storage space hangs Cash's collection of crosses and crucifixes. "I just mix different ages of crosses," she says. "The one on the extreme left is contemporary and made of barbed wire and wood." Across the hall, a Mexican painting of Saint John looks over several santos, crowns, and one of Cash's earliest pieces, an early-seventeenth-century santo with flowing robes in gold and red.

Cash initially wanted her house to be simply in tune with Spanish Colonial style and the Santa Fe landscape, but she ended up with something much more personal and meaningful. "Life goes on," she notes. "I had my bout with cancer and my broken back. This house is a testa-ment to my survival and a day-to-day balm to my spirits."

RICHLY LAYERED

A Texan treasure trove and an artful village south of the border

FORT WORTH, TEXAS, AND SAN MIGUEL DE ALLENDE, MEXICO

LEGENDARY HOMES ARE THE PURVIEW of Martha Hyder, a legend herself in the international worlds of collecting, classical music, and society. Fort Worth, Texas, and San Miguel de Allende, Mexico, are Hyder's main resting points, and the two homes are studies in eclectic decorating of the highest order. In the United States, it's gilded French and Italian furniture, Russian icons, santos, and putti galore, while Mexico gets an artisanal approach to a ten-bedroom villa.

Nowadays Hyder spends most of her time in the comfort of her Fort Worth home surrounded by her favorite objects that she and her late husband, Elton Hyder Jr., collected. Mr. Hyder, a lawyer and real estate developer, became famous at age twenty-eight for being the youngest attorney general in Texas, for serving as an attorney at the war crimes trial of Japanese Prime Minister Hideki Tojo, and eventually for transforming the Tarlton Law Library at the University of Texas at Austin with more than four thousand artifacts he amassed. It is easy to see that they both shared a deep love of history and the arts. Brimming with pride, daughter Whitney Moore points out Victorian Lord High Chancellor's purses, which were used in the opening of the British Parliament ceremonies, that her father collected. And when asked about the multitudes of Russian icons, she responded, "Mother went through an icon phase," as if it were the most normal thing in the world.

That icon period grew out of Martha Hyder's interest in the Russian music scene when she was closely involved with the founding of the Van Cliburn International Piano Competition. As president of the foundation in the mid-1970s, Hyder brought worldwide attention to the competition held every four years in Fort Worth. "At one point, Mother became very close to Vladimir Viardo, a winner of the competition," says Moore. "At the time we were traveling frequently to the Soviet Union, and he became like family. Nothing was too difficult for Mother; when his family needed a new windshield for their car, she bought one, packed it up, and dropped it off on her

PREVIOUS SPREAD:

Rich reds, golds, and yellows set the tone for the Fort Worth drawing room. The English Bible stand to the left of the marble mantel supports a vintage embroidered velvet pillow while the one at right has an elaborately bound antique Bible. In front of the fireplace is an eighteenth-century stool with cut-velvet upholstery.

OPPOSITE:

ABOVE LEFT: A painted eighteenth-century Italian chest fades into the boiseries of the foyer.

ABOVE RIGHT: Seventeenth- and eighteenth-century Italian putti on an antique Italian bureau.

BELOW RIGHT: Smaller Russian icons flank a large icon of the Madonna and child that was purchased from the estate of Florence Gould. The crown above is Peruvian. The candlesticks are Colonial silver from South America.

BELOW LEFT: A pair of seventeenth-century Mexican carved wood skeletons amid eighteenth-century Italian candlesticks.

next trip there. She was like Santa Claus!" That sort of generosity was atypical at a time when Americans and Soviets looked upon each other with suspicion, and trade between the two countries barely existed. The icons, however, were purchased legally, mostly in the auction salesrooms of London and New York. Topped with a Peruvian folk art crown, a notably large icon from the estate of famed collector Florence Gould depicts the Madonna and child in gilded splendor. Under a rock crystal chandelier in her glittering dining room at the ends of a long mahogany table is one of Hyder's prized possessions from this period of collecting: a pair of jewel-studded crowns that were offered to Czar Nicholas II and Alexandra of Russia as wedding gifts.

Built in 1916, the Fort Worth mansion was given a three-year renovation by Hyder starting in 1959, when the couple purchased it. "Mother went through the house room by room," Moore comments. "She transformed it from an English Tudor revival to her fantasy of an Italian villa." Filling the house with objects was not a great trouble to Hyder, who loves collecting and putting rooms together. Late-eighteenth-century English pull dogs—they bark when you pull the cord—poke out from under a gilded stool in the paneled library. Sharing space with the playful iron pugs are seventeenth-century Mexican skulls meant to remind the faithful in church of our limited time on this earth.

More devotional art fills the sunny yellow drawing room. Setting the tone in the room, a gilt Regency bureau stands at the entrance topped with four seventeenth-century Italian putti, or angels, each holding a candle and dancing around a crucifix in the middle. Flanking the fireplace, a pair of nineteenth-century easels support an antique Bible and a gold-thread-embroidered pillow fit for a papal nap.

A big believer in sharing the wealth of her life, Hyder is known for the frequent events she has held in her Fort Worth home. Opening the house to many non-profit institutions such as the Fort Worth Symphony, Fort Worth Ballet, and the Fort Worth Museum of Art is simply a part of her being. Representing more than four decades of collecting from all over the globe, this houseful of treasures is a testament to a richly lived existence.

The two smaller crowns on the Georgian mahogany dining table were reputedly gifts to the last czar of Russia. Distinctive Irish Chippendale chairs surround the dining table. Over the eighteenth-century English pine fireplace hangs a silver-thread religious panel that has tarnished over time.

Martha Hyder's San Miguel de Allende house more than measures up to her Texan residence albeit in a slightly more casual manner. The house is in the middle of the city, but a wall along the edge of the property conceals it from its neighbors. It is not, as one might imagine, a plain wall. In the world of Martha Hyder, nothing is plain. More façade or stage set than wall, this perimeter border is stuccoed and trimmed to look like different buildings one might find in a Mexican town. "That is supposed to be an arsenal," explains Moore, "and that portion over there is like a villa—there just isn't any inside! This is one of the charms of Mexico, the craftsmen here can make anything look old." A double staircase wraps around a turquoise tile-lined pool that is actually a hot tub. Helping take the hard edge off the masonry is cissus, a Virginia creeper–like climber, and creeping fig, which clamber over every surface.

In 1959, the Hyders bought a building that sounds as though it was more like a garage than a home, with a machine shop and rumors of pigs and donkeys having been in what is now the living room. The purchase of several other adjacent lots led to the creation of this hacienda called Quinta Quebrada, or broken farm, due to the neglected state of the street. In the late 1980s, a serious remodeling effort was started. The house now boasts ten bedrooms, eleven baths, and several kitchens. "Mother told Father she just needed to expand the kitchen a bit and add a bathroom. Look what we got!" jokes Moore. "She just built and built, until Father said enough is enough and refused to return until the

OPPOSITE:

Indian and Moroccan fabrics lend an exotic flair to Hyder's living room in San Miguel de Allende. An Italian eighteenth-century mirror hangs over the fireplace, which is original to the house.

FOLLOWING SPREAD:

LEFT PAGE, ABOVE LEFT: Antique priests' vestments and bullfighting suits share wall space in the library, which opens onto a courtyard. On the landing, the English painting of a judge is part of the late Elton Hyder Jr.'s collection of legal art and artifacts.

LEFT PAGE, ABOVE RIGHT: Displayed between two gilded altar pieces is a traveling Mexican retablo; angels painted on the inside of the doors flank the Nativity scene inside.

LEFT PAGE, BELOW: Columns with Corinthian capitals, salvaged from a Mexican church, form the bed in the master bedroom. As elsewhere in the house, the two Moroccan tables in the foreground have intricate mother-of-pearl inlay.

RIGHT PAGE, ABOVE: The large silver candlesticks in the dining room were copied from a Guatemalan original. Above the buffet, an antique triptych depicts the Crucifixion of Christ.

RIGHT PAGE, BELOW RIGHT: A small altarlike vignette composed of bouquet-wielding cherubs sitting on upturned capitals, turned wood candlesticks, and gold-embroidered ecclesiastical textiles.

RIGHT PAGE, BELOW LEFT: Acting as an outdoor living room, the loggia is decorated in the same manner as the interior. Here, a large gilt-wood *resplendor* hangs above an antique santo in a silk gown.

rebuilding was completed." When he did return, it was to a magical hideaway home filled with a wide assortment of art, antiques, and textiles.

Between the two pairs of French doors that lead to the living room from the loggia, a marble-topped, wrought-iron console holds an eighteenth-century santo in a silk dress. Behind her an antique mirror reflects the greenery outside and above that the golden rays of a large Peruvian *resplendor*. In the living room, Indian and Morrocan fabrics draped over sofas and ottomans and covering pillows attest to the less formal style of the house. A Moroccan lantern along with several altar candlesticks illuminate the room. Specially designed for the room is an Aubusson-style rug woven in San Miguel de Allende; it picks up the colors found there. In the pale yellow library, the display is even more disparate. Matador suits share wall space with antique priest vestments and an antique English painting of a judge.

Even the bedrooms, which could have been a bit more neutral, manifest the Hyder touch. Two of them share a pale blue, brown, and coral color scheme, but the similarities end there. In the master bedroom, the bed, which boasts a painted architectural fragment on the headboard, is lavishly curtained in linen, its corners marked by tall antique church columns. "When she first bought this house, nobody collected these things," says Moore. "She almost didn't have to leave the house; people would just show up with objects to sell. Luckily she just bought and bought and put it all in storage till she was ready to redo the house." Made of four antique gilded wood panels joined in a stepped pattern, the headboard in the other pale blue bedroom looks like a choir stall. One pair of old church doors were set with mirrors in the paneling and now serve as closet doors.

As with her home in Fort Worth, Quinta Quebrada has been turned into a center of the community by Martha Hyder. Everyone seems to know of the house and its intriguing owner. Although a more casual spirit led the decorating here than in Fort Worth, it is still a product of Hyder's interest in the arts and history. In reviving and expanding a structure that dates back to the eighteenth century, Hyder has created a home for family and friends that is filled with her personality. Both properties feature her eclectic style, a true reflection of a legendary couple engaged with the world.

The patio is a pastiche of different styles meant to evoke an older structure. The bench on the far wall was copied from an English original.

In the home of Alvin Friedman-Kien, a fifteenth-century Italian walnut table supports a contemporary piece of art glass by Dale Chihuly and a gilded sculptural portrait of a Tibetan monk.

AN ARTFUL MIX

ART AND ANTIQUES

Six millennia of antiques and contemporary art in a Manhattan duplex

NEW YORK, NEW YORK

"I STARTED COLLECTING AT THREE, with marbles, stamps at seven, coins at nine, and Oriental carpets at eleven!" claims Alvin Friedman-Kien. Building on a precocious childhood, this successful New York City dermatologist used that early training to his duplex apartment's advantage, with a mini museum's worth of artwork from the Neolithic age to today. Ming cabinets, a Chippendale chaise, and Jules LeLeu tub chairs mingle with a plethora of sacred objects from cultures around the world. Top-notch quality ties it all together. "There is no specific thing that I collect," Friedman-Kien says. "I collect as I find things I like."

Upon entering the apartment, one is faced with a multipanel screen of cranes on a gold ground. This eighteenth-century Japanese piece belonged to the Tokugowa family, prominent samurais in the seventeenth and eighteenth centuries who established the Edo shogunate, a 250-year period of stability in Japan. The screen imparts the same sense of peace that is found throughout the apartment.

With its attractive arched windows, the living room contains many of Friedman-Kien's treasures. Between two pairs of windows hangs a large crayon drawing in several shades of blue by present-day artist Cy Twombly. This 1972 work on paper is typical of many Twombly created, with an abstract drawn line, much like cursive writing, which marks the moment of its creation. In contrast to the Twombly, a nearby twelfth-century Indian Shiva bronze stands on a sixteenth-century Ming altar table.

This mix of contemporary art with highly religious art makes one look at both with a fresh eye.

In the sitting area by the fireplace the eclectic theme of the apartment continues with an Irish Chippendale chaise and a glass coffee table that acts as a protective cover to a massive pair of stucco feet from a second- or third-century Gandahara Buddha. Ming cabinets frame the fireplace; one features a mounted Neolithic period bi-disc, used in funerary rites, and the other displays a ceramic sculpture by Friedman-Kien's partner, Ryo Toyonaga, who explores the friction between man

PREVIOUS SPREAD:

A sixteenth-century Thai Buddha head complements the Chinese sixteenth-century Ming chairs in huanghuali, an extinct type of rosewood.

OPPOSITE:

ABOVE LEFT: A six-panel Japanese religious screen illustrates the descent of Buddha.

ABOVE RIGHT: A bronze twelfth-century Chola Shiva from India.

BELOW RIGHT: Hanging in the guest bedroom, this intricate Indian painting represents a god who is always shown with blue faces, surrounded by cows of several different colors.

BELOW LEFT: A pair of pre-Khmer Cambodian sculptures: on the left is Uma and to the right is Shiva.

A large Cy Twombly 1972 crayon-on-paper drawing in various shades of blue dominates the living room. The four circa-1930 wood-trimmed tub chairs are by Jules LeLeu, a noted French cabinetmaker of the Art Deco period. Above the fireplace is a canvas sculpture by Lee Bontecou. To the right of the fireplace is a Ming cabinet with a ceramic by Ryo Toyonaga, who also sculpted the piece on the left side of the altar table under the Twombly.

and nature in his biomorphic artwork. "The mixture is what it is all about," Friedman-Kien says, in explaining the placement and the varied nature of his collection.

True to his statement about simply owning objects he likes is the jade-green bedroom. On top of a Queen Anne English walnut dresser sits a metal object Friedman-Kien identifies as an actual spigot from a beer barrel. It may not find its way to the Metropolitan Museum of Art, like so many of the apartment's pieces could, but someone designed this hardware with care, and Friedman-Kien appreciates it for its form and patina. Beside the spigot is a seventeenth-century French marble head. A large eighteenth-century Italian carved-wood mirror hangs behind this eclectic mix of objects.

"You can live with these pieces," Friedman-Kien says. "I think it is important to view modern artworks in this environment. It makes one see them in a different light." Indeed this is certainly not a white cube gallery space but rather an exploration of one man's far-flung interests. Here a Ming altar table may look brand-new, or a contemporary Lee Bontecou canvas sculpture can draw parallels to ancient works of art. "I believe that collectors are born, not made," Friedman-Kien comments. "These artworks enrich my life enormously."

Standing between two windows, a life-size Cambodian tenth-century Hindu god is immediately visible as one enters the living room. To the left is a bronze piece of African currency and to the right another tenth-century Cambodian sculpture of Uma, a Hindu goddess.

A GENEROUS HEART

A sharp eye for Modern masters reflecting the soul of the southwest

TESUQUE, NEW MEXICO

A CHARITABLE HEART RULES over this art-filled house in Tesuque, New Mexico. Its owners created and now run a foundation that aids children in Africa. As the wife says, "I am attuned to suffering and conflict in my work life; when I get home, I want a calming atmosphere. I look for pieces that speak to me, that show humanity in the faces." The objects she has collected range from pioneering modernist works of art rooted in the southwest to santos and other pieces of devotional art.

Aside from giving her the peace she craves, the objects also reflect her interests from a spiritual perspective. "I'm not a very traditional Christian, and I wasn't raised in the Catholic Church, so santos don't have as much religious meaning as they might to others; it's a bit more neutral for me," she states. "On the whole, though,

PREVIOUS SPREAD:

Above the fireplace in the living room hangs Georgia O'Keeffe's *Black Place II,* an oil on canvas from 1945. The homeowner purchased the box with the angels on it in France. It originally held communion wafers.

RIGHT:

Polished brick floors line the front hall. A late-nineteenth-century Zia storage jar crowns the table by the door at left. A pair of nineteenth-century northern New Mexican jars flank the front door. Kenneth Adams's *Indian Odalisque,* circa 1920, hangs above the antique South American bench.

our religious objects are deeply meaningful to me and evoke a connection to my faith and our local community."

A more European flavor permeated the house when the couple first bought it from the previous owner, decorator Barbara Windom. Initially they bought several pieces from Windom, then began decorating on their own.

The homeowner, who professes to have loved arranging objects since childhood, was a natural at combining key elements in her new environment. A strong historical and spiritual thread runs through the house, she says. "I love the art of composition, arranging things until they feel 'right.' It is one of the most satisfying things in the world, as well as calming." A group of three archangels from Guatemala were separated, and each now holds court individually, set back in the deeply recessed window niches along with a bronze altar candlestick. In the front hall an array of quintessentially southwestern arts and crafts line the brick-floored space. Above an antique South American bench hangs Kenneth Adams's *Indian Odalisque*, circa 1920, depicting a reclining Native American woman, and on the bench lies a pair of blankets—one with a serrated diamond pattern, called a saltillo-style Germantown Rio Grande, from the late nineteenth century, and the other a circa-1870 Navajo woman's wearing blanket in the late classic style, woven of homespun wool enhanced with cochineal and indigo dyes.

The homeowner collaborated with interior designer Jane Smith on the interior of her 1989 adobe house, especially the living room, master bedroom, studio, and outdoor portal. She attributes the final look of the house to Windom, Smith, and herself. "This was really a collaboration among the three of us. Both Jane and Barbara brought a lot to this project." Although quite confident in her instincts, Smith's client felt the need to hire a design professional who could give her more access to furniture, fabrics, and local craftsmen. "This is the home of a wonderful client with a great eye," Smith proclaims. "Her training in fine art and interest in the human condition inform all her purchases." Paisley pillows, patchwork quilts on the beds, and Native American textiles contribute to the sense of history and connection to place that the client sought to establish.

A noteworthy collection of nineteenth- and twentieth-century American art by southwestern painters enlivens the house. Over the living room fireplace hangs a 1945 Georgia O'Keeffe oil, *Black Place II*, which the homeowner sought out because it represents the area so well. Started in 1943, the *Black Place* series of paintings depicts sacred Native American lands at a favorite painting spot O'Keeffe called Black Place, near her home in Ghost Ranch, New Mexico. Another local scene is shown in *Indian Fishing with Horse Hair*, by E. Martin Hennings, a member of the Taos Society of Artists. Marsden Hartley's *Camellias No. 1*, painted in 1920, graces the wall of the breakfast room. The homeowner calls it one of Hartley's happier paintings. Together with several other works of art, both devotional and secular, these paintings ground this Tesuque home in the local environment.

Santos like this Virgin Mary were originally dressed with elaborate gowns, hence their lack of lower limbs. This contemporary look works well in the spare space.

MIXED MEDIA

Select pieces bring serenity to a light-filled artist's studio

NEW YORK, NEW YORK

It is hard to imagine Santa Fe style in Manhattan without thinking of 1980s kitsch, but fashion world insider turned photographer Kelly Klein has conceived an elegant space with a nod to the southwest. Known for her minimal take on fashion and photography, Klein combined art and antiques from several different eras with textures and, most important, a great amount of light to create an ode to casual luxe. With help from her mother, Santa Fe gallerist Gloria List, Klein selected a few devotional artifacts to complement her spare interior. Even on the cloudiest of days, Klein's two-story space overlooking Central Park West glows with warmth from her patinated objects.

"My mother introduced me to devotional art when she started dealing years ago," Klein says. "I collect things because I like them, not because of what they are or their perceived value." In one corner of her living room sits an eighteenth-century statue of the Virgin Mary holding the Christ child. Rare embroidered white gowns dress the two, giving the pair a regal air. List explains that she bought the piece in Portugal, but that it is difficult to tell if the costumes are original. "They are in extraordinary condition, so it is hard to believe that they might be three hundred years old. But it is interesting to see the figures fully dressed, as one might have in a church or private home."

Between the two Belgian linen–covered sofas, a large coffee table acts as a platform for a pair of disparate sculptures. One is a nude marble figure of Aphrodite from eighteenth-century Italy that may have been made as a grand tour souvenir, from that era when rich Englishmen traveled the globe collecting artworks and displaying them as symbols of their worldliness and wealth. For contrast, Klein has juxtaposed it with a Guatemalan santo with articulated arms, most probably to allow it to be dressed in a similar manner to Klein's nearby Madonna. "I can't really tell who she is because she didn't come with a dress," List notes. "Oftentimes the costume or the objects that a santo might be holding give one an idea of who is being represented."

A modern sculpture by Juan Hamilton, in the shape of an oversize pebble, graces the living room, adding a Zenlike quality to the room. Hamilton, who works in bronze and ceramic, is a New Mexican sculptor best known as Georgia O'Keeffe's studio assistant during the last years of the artist's life. In 1973, as a young man, Hamilton moved to New Mexico and began working

PREVIOUS SPREAD:

A double-height casement window illuminates this studio-like apartment. Jean-Michel Frank–style leather chairs and linen-upholstered sofas continue the streamlined look. In the foreground is a sculpture by Juan Hamilton, a New Mexican ceramicist.

OPPOSITE:

On the coffee table is an eighteenth-century Italian marble statue of Aphrodite, the Greek goddess of love and beauty. A blue-painted Guatemalan santo stands nearby.

KELLY KLEIN

for O'Keeffe, encouraging her to resume her artwork despite her near-blindness. He came to his own imagery, which recalls the art of modern masters in its minimalism, via his work restoring a traditional adobe house in Santa Fe and, as he says, from something deep within that guides and inspires him.

"It is really just a beautiful object to look at," Klein says, referring to the Hamilton. Each of the particularly fine sculptures in the living room, illuminated by the large art studio–like casement windows, speaks to Klein on a personal, spiritual level. This smattering of valued objects casually placed about the atelier-like living room gives the impression that the resident is a sophisticated woman in touch with her inner spirit.

Klein's mother, Gloria List, purchased this large eighteenth-century Madonna and child in Oirique, Portugal; the gowns they are wearing are most probably from a later date.

WORLD CITIZENS

Celebrating Jewish culture amid an international selection of modern masters

EASTERN PENNSYLVANIA

WORLDLY TREASURES FILL this East Coast art collector's loftlike apartment, ranging from African artifacts to ceramics by Picasso to Judaica the couple acquired around the world. Paintings by Hans Hoffmann, Josef Albers, and William Glackens surround the dining area, along with sculptures by Alberto Giacometti, Henry Moore, and Alexander Calder. The living room boasts an equally impressive roster of artwork, including pieces by Jean Dubuffet, Fernand Léger, Alice Neel, Jacques Lipschitz, and David Hockney. "We have always enjoyed art and have always collected," the wife explains. "Over the years we developed affinities for certain periods and artists—particularly early modern and Judaica."

Clearly this family appreciates living with their art and treats it as a normal part of their lives. Their Judaica collection in particular allows them to interact with these objects on a regular basis. For the most part, the dreidels, menorahs, and kiddush cups are also used in the family's religious rituals. More important, these pieces represent the many areas of the globe where Jews developed communities and therefore connect the family to their view of Judaism. As the wife explains, "Jewish ritual objects often incorporated the visual influence of the surrounding culture, and the Judaica we collect comes from all the corners of the world Jews made home." Kiddush cups, used at weekly Sabbath dinners, and dreidels, part of a game children play during Hanukkah, seem to be the objects found most frequently on the couple's journeys.

"We are very much a people of the world and love to travel. I think that is a major part of the Jewish experience. There is something inspiring about a religious tradition so focused on ethical human behavior that it survived and thrived over millennia in so many places. We like being links in that chain," she says.

Their silver kiddush cups, displayed on a shelf between Asian ceramics and a Picasso pottery plate, are always close at hand. At the Sabbath dinner, a commandment in the Torah requires that the kiddush prayer be recited and the wine blessed. The kiddush cup is then passed for all to drink from, or in some cases poured into smaller individual cups. This couple's collection of kiddush cups comes from Germany, Israel, Iran, and Russia.

PREVIOUS SPREAD:

The wide windowsill allows for the display of menorahs and contemporary sculptures. Hanging from the ceiling is a 1950 mobile by Alexander Calder; just below it is a Malaysian stool with a cocoa grater.

OPPOSITE:

ABOVE LEFT: A Picasso ceramic with a menorah by Shraga Landesman to the left and one by Ari Sidler to the right.
ABOVE RIGHT: The Rampant Lions of Judah, a symbol of the Israelite tribe of Judah, support a traditional menorah.
BELOW: A view of the dining area with William Glackens's *New England Landscape* above the buffet, a Josef Albers *Homage to the Square* painting to the left, and a Senufo bird sculpture to the right.

Opening on to the balcony, the spacious living room boasts an impressive array of artworks. At left is Jean Dubuffet's 1971 sculpture *Papa Les Savantes* and on the sofa table is *Bather,* 1968, by Jacques Lipschitz. Just beyond the sofa is a Degas ballerina in bronze. A collection of shofars sits on the coffee table; these ram horns are blown on the holiday of Rosh Hashanah.

The dreidels, on the other hand, come out only once a year, during Hanukkah, when the children play Spin the Dreidel, a game of chance. The sides of the dreidel bear letters from the Hebrew alphabet, making an anagram of the phrase "A great miracle happened here." Each letter is worth a certain amount. After spinning the dreidel, each player either puts money in or takes money out of the pot, depending on how the dreidel falls. "In our family, everyone puts a portion of their winnings in one of the tzedakah boxes," the homeowner explains. "Then the children choose what good cause to support with their donation. I look at the dreidel as a metaphor for the element of chance in our lives."

Objects from other cultures have a more decorative nature in this home, but still represent the craftsmen who produced them. Amid all of these early modern artworks, two Senufo pieces from Côte d'Ivoire serve as a reminder of the African artworks that inspired Picasso and other early-twentieth-century artists. A symbol of fertility, the large Senufo bird that stands in the corner of the dining area, bearing both male and female attributes, emphasizes the necessity of the two genders to continue Senufo society. The Senufo stool used to wash laundry is more utilitarian. Its thick tapering legs allowed women to set it in shallow water to scrub their garments on its surface.

Nothing in this home is locked in place; new combinations give the owners a different outlook on their collections. "I am constantly moving pieces," the wife says. "It's good to shake things up." Living with all this art, and constant exposure to new ideas and new cultures, plays an important role in the lives of these homeowners, who look at their Jewish history as a crucial part of their identity. "Art is all about seeing," the wife says, explaining their eclectic collections. "The pleasure of art is that it makes you see the world in a different way."

OPPOSITE:

ABOVE LEFT: An international collection of silver kiddush cups, which are regularly used on the Sabbath.

ABOVE RIGHT: A silver bowl with sequined dreidels from India shares space on a credenza with a sculpture by Joan Miró and a Fernand Léger painting.

BELOW RIGHT: Silver dreidels from around the world.

BELOW LEFT: In the living room bookcase are silver kiddush cups from Russia, Germany, Israel, and Iran and a ceramic plate by Picasso.

MINIMALISM AND COMFORT

A jeweler explores the world, finding inspiration in ancient cultures

DALLAS, TEXAS

Two ends of the visual spectrum, elaborate and minimal, meld seamlessly in Carol Taylor's Dallas home. As a former gallerist, Taylor embraced the minimalists of the 1960s and '70s in her gallery, while also enjoying and collecting religious works of art that had meaning for her. With its pale walls and subdued lighting, her home is a manifestation of her interests. A large Robert Mangold drawing may dominate one wall, but close by, a collection of religious artifacts from cultures around the world demands closer inspection.

Exhibiting modern art in her Dallas gallery, opened in 1980, may not have been the wisest business move, but Taylor loved the artworks and was not deterred. "I opened the gallery with a Bruce Nauman show of his little circle drawings, and the [security] alarm went off the first night," Taylor recounts. "When I met the policeman at the gallery, he asked me incredulously if I thought anyone was going to steal these pieces! I kept at it for six years, showing artists like Richard Serra, Sol LeWitt, and Robert Mangold. It went over like a lead balloon, but it was great fun, and the artists liked coming here."

PREVIOUS SPREAD:

Gilt rays emanate from a dramatic three-foot-tall Ecuadorean crucifix in the living room.

RIGHT:

Minimalist artworks, including a large Robert Mangold over the sofa, share space with an international array of devotional art in Taylor's living room. Above the fireplace is *Circle in Mexico* by Richard Long, a British land artist.

Now a jeweler who designs pieces using antique and vintage beads, Taylor explains the beginning of her second career: "I started off simply wanting a long jade necklace and went to a Chinese shop and bought some old beads and had them strung together. One thing led to another and I found myself designing jewelry for a living." From exhibiting underappreciated artists to creating jewelry she herself would wear, Taylor keeps true to herself. Her Dallas home bears witness to worldwide travels sourcing beads and artifacts for her business. Objects such as the coral-and-turquoise-encrusted Mani, or Buddhist prayer wheel, have a quiet beauty that appeals to Taylor in the same way as her minimalist artworks. The Mani contains many copies of a written prayer, or mantra. Each time it is swung, the prayers spin inside and a new blessing is spread silently. "I just wonder how many people have sent out prayers with this?" Taylor remarks. "Simply twirling it is a quiet wish for well-being."

Taylor's respect for the creations of others extends to their cultural lifestyle and history. Explaining the signifi-cance of a Tuareg cross, made in Agadez, Mali, which protects its wearer, Taylor expands on her appreciation of the landscape where she bought the piece. "I came across a Tuareg encampment in Mali, which was just a romantic visual explosion. They are true nomads, and there in the Sahara you still see many of them in their traditional indigo robes. And when I went to Timbuktu, an important stop on the salt trade route, it was spectacular to witness such an ancient, sophisticated culture, with libraries, mosques, and universities that go back so many centuries."

Taylor's confident, eclectic style allows for her tribal and devotional pieces to coexist with her minimal art-works. Above the headboard in her master bedroom, favorite pieces are displayed in an almost gridlike forma-tion. A pair of gilded architectural fragments from her mother center the composition. Below them are retablos of Saint Joaquin and Saint Francis. A pair of early-1800s Venetian gilt-wood palmettos, probably used on the top of a ceremonial staff, cross each other between the two por-traits. Little crosses are interspersed among the objects on the wall. "I've been collecting crosses for over twenty years now," Taylor says. "I am just fascinated by religious art. There is something very alluring to me about how these pieces have been used over the centuries and the different belief systems that they represent." On one corner of the wall, just above the pillows, hangs a pair of silver ex-votos with breasts, gifts to Taylor from friends after she survived two bouts with breast cancer. "They may not have saved my life," Taylor says of the ex-votos, "but as symbols of support and hope, they mean so much to me."

OPPOSITE:

ABOVE LEFT: Turquoise, coral, and lapis lazuli decorate a bone-handled Buddhist prayer wheel.

ABOVE RIGHT: A silver finial for a processional staff purchased in Buenos Aires.

BELOW RIGHT: Nestled in antique branch coral, which Taylor uses in her jewelry, is a South American silver crucifix pendant.

BELOW LEFT: The lacelike patterns of these nickel silver processional crosses are typical of Coptic patterns.

SPANISH SETTING

Treasures from Latin America shine against warm colors

SANTA BARBARA, CALIFORNIA

Thirty-eight years dealing in devotional art has left Michael Haskell with an enviable private cache of art and antiques. In the beginning he concentrated on Native American objects in his Montecito, California, gallery and shop, but over the years he has refocused his speciality on the arts of Latin America. Haskell says, "I enjoyed the trips to Mexico and South America, and seeing the antiques in their original context. It is harder to find good material there now, but every once in a while a friend will call me from Peru with a great find from some old family."

As Haskell explains, most of his objects came from the Spanish viceroyalties located in Colombia, Mexico, and Peru. These colonies of Spain were remarkably wealthy from the gold and silver trade and, beginning in the sixteenth century, became centers of power, culture, and religion. The Cuzqueño school of painting sprouted up in Cuzco, Peru, where Spanish missionaries taught Mestizos, those of mixed Spanish and native background, how to paint in the European manner. However, the local Peruvian painters eventually developed a style that incorporated their own visual vocabulary. The resulting paintings, mostly of religious subjects such as the Virgin Mary, the Holy Family, and the Crucifixion, have become quite sought-after artworks. One of Haskell's examples of Cuzqueño painting is a Madonna nursing the Christ child. It hangs in his dining room, among several other Colonial-era paintings, with subjects ranging from a virgin who was walled up in the twelfth century to the patron saint of Mexico, the Virgin of Guadalupe.

Other Latin American artifacts are scattered throughout the house and incorporated into the architecture. The entrance to the home features several noteworthy items built right into the structure. Two eighteenth-century Peruvian columns flanking the front door support the overhang, creating a front porch. Eighteenth-century Mexican doors made of long-lasting sabino (water cypress)

PREVIOUS SPREAD:

The rich color of the pigmented plaster walls and the Saltillo tile floors provide a distinctive background to this assembly of antiques. A collection of Puebla pottery sits atop the green eighteenth-century Peruvian table. The smaller ceramic objects are antique inkwells and sanders for spilled ink. The *frailero,* or monk's chair, with the tooled leather seat and back originates from the same period. Below the table, an 1820 painted barrel complements the tones of the room.

OPPOSITE:

ABOVE LEFT: A Mexican folk-art shelf with an eagle on the back panel holds an eighteenth-century Peruvian silver chalice and baptismal shell. On the wall is a pair of processional crosses, which would have been mounted on staffs.

ABOVE RIGHT: A Mexican ex-voto depicts a church with collapsing scaffolding and a dead worker on the ground and one hanging on for dear life. Presumably, this was offered in thanks by the man who lived.

BELOW RIGHT: The living room contains an eighteenth-century Peruvian cupboard with Puebla pottery. The three pieces at right are from Tonala, a center of Mexican ceramics since pre-Columbian times. The eighteenth-century Mexican painting depicts the Crucifixion.

BELOW LEFT: Eighteenth-century silver reliquary pendants with patron saints painted on copper.

Bright green trim on the dining room doorways complements the chairs from Mallorca, Spain, and the large painted cupboard at the back. Eighteenth- to early-twentieth-century serving trays with lacquered floral decorations, called *bateas,* hang high on the walls. Haskell designed the imposing wrought-iron chandelier that illuminates the room.

wood greet visitors to Haskell's home. Above the door a Virgin carved of cantero stone, a Mexican material often used for sculpture, is ensconced in an arched blue niche. And the entrance is illuminated by a pair of eighteenth-century Mexican carriage lamps. All this is just an introduction to the treasures displayed within the house.

Haskell built the residence twenty-six years ago, in a hybrid of California Mediterranean and Mexican styles. Brightly colored rooms arranged around a central courtyard hold Haskell's collections. The dining room, which has the feel of a great hall, with its large fireplace and exposed wooden rafters, is dominated by the large eighteenth-century-style Mexican chandelier. Surrounding the eighteenth-century Spanish Colonial table, traditional ladder-back chairs with rush seats from Mallorca, Spain, match the room's teal blue window and door frames. A Mexican ex-voto painting resting on a chair from Michoacán, Mexico, depicts a man giving thanks to God for sparing his life, while his companion, who has fallen off scaffolding, lies dead on the ground. An elabo-

rate Peruvian corona, an architectural fragment typically used as a decorative transom, tops one of the room's doors.

Terra-cotta-colored plaster walls warm the cozy living room filled with antiques, and a large cantero stone fireplace that Haskell commissioned thirty years ago stands at the ready for a roaring fire. At either side of the room, pottery-topped storage pieces illustrate the difference between a traditional *trastero* and a more formal armoire. The *trastero* is an eighteenth-century Peruvian cupboard meant to hold most anything but clothes. The doweled front allowed for air circulation, which was particularly important if food was kept within. The elaborately carved armoire across the living room, also from the eighteenth century, is made from Mexican sabino wood. This type of furniture was used for holding folded garments; the care taken in the carving and use of a rare wood indicates that the piece came from a wealthy household that had clothing worth protecting.

Along with mixing vintage textiles and many other artworks and antiques, Haskell has created a home environment that reflects his career as a dealer. He doesn't collect just pictures of the Virgin but also the special little retablo that depicts Pascal Baylon, the patron saint of cooks, and a rare version of Santa Filomena, a young martyr of the early Catholic Church, who is shown as a girl bearing a bouquet of lilies. Whether at home or in his gallery, Haskell is a natural-born raconteur who enjoys telling the story of these paintings or explaining the original use of an antique to the benefit of friends, colleagues, and clients alike.

OPPOSITE:

ABOVE LEFT: A Peruvian eighteenth-century gilt-wood shelf placed over a doorway holds a crucifix and Mexican and Peruvian coffers.

ABOVE RIGHT: Framed in tin, the Mexican retablo above the Peruvian wall-mounted shelf shows the Virgin Mary as Our Lady of Charity, with a white dove symbolizing the Holy Spirit.

BELOW: The headboard in the master bedroom is actually an eighteenth-century altar balustrade. Hawaiian koa wood bowls sit atop an early-eighteenth-century Spanish dowry chest. A suzani is used as a coverlet.

A side table in Cece Cord's New York apartment displays a pair of crosses amid a selection of silver bibelots.

A DECORATIVE NOTE

FAITH IN ART

Ecclesiastical art brings spiritual comfort to the home

HOUSTON, TEXAS

"THE ART I COLLECT ISN'T SO MUCH about a trend as much as it is about my faith and the things that I grew up with," comments Sallie Ann Hart. Although she doesn't describe herself as religious—she prefers the term *spiritual*—she finds that she is drawn to ecclesiastical art. "One has to glean from religion or faith what one needs. I'm not that devout, and I'm not warding off evil spirits with these objects. They just are beautiful to me."

The vivid persimmon red of Hart's dining room in Houston, Texas, sums up her connection to her art collection: "Some people like comfort food; I happen to like comfort art." Growing up Catholic, Hart found quiet solace in the Church and looked to the saints and Holy Family as friends with whom she could communicate. Her collection of South American primitive crosses, some with a papal crown on top, originate from a church

PREVIOUS SPREAD:

These markers of the Stations of the Cross stand out against the persimmon-red painted walls of the dining room. At the center of the console is an Italian gilt tabernacle, originally meant to hold the Eucharist.

OPPOSITE:

The arched painting of the Madonna and child echoes the arches of the French doors and bookcases in the garden room. The blue and white awning stripe on the upholstered furniture complements the painting and the santo standing on the side table. Between the French doors is part of Hart's collection of heraldic crests.

where they were used to designate the Stations of the Cross. On a console, Hart placed an ornate gilded tabernacle with a carved marble Christ child. And by an arched window stands a sixty-light, wrought-iron votive holder straight out of a church. "I don't light candles for people! But it does look awfully pretty lit up at night with the glowing reflections in the window."

Throughout the house are several altars or, as Hart says, what decorators would call vignettes. There is even one for the family dog, located near his food and bowls. "As in Europe, here in the southwest it is more acceptable to collect this sort of art. When we lived in Georgetown my friends thought I was a bit off!" In this setting, though, each piece looks totally at home, be it a gilded crown as a coffee table accent or the very sculptural Virgin and child from Mexico in the garden room. Hart explains that the house, designed by her husband, Bob, an energy executive turned architect, inspired her to collect even more religious art. The garden room's arches, for example, are a perfect complement to the primitive Madonna and child painted on an arched wooden board hanging over the fireplace.

Together the two have created a home filled with art and antiques that soothes the soul and fills the heart.

Traditionally, Catholic congregants light candles in churches in votive holders like this one and pray for the ill or deceased. Now Hart lights the little candles for illumination at night and appreciates their flicker in the window.

TEXAS ROSE

Mirrors and candles create a Provençal glow

HOUSTON, TEXAS

A LOVE FOR FLOWERS AND CANDLELIGHT could easily overpower a house, but for Houston decorator Carol Glasser, they simply set the tone. "I'm a romantic," Glasser explains as she surveys her surroundings. "It's hard to find charm here. We don't have a lot of age in Houston, and I've tried to add a layer of history with my antiques and santos." Building character into a room is Glasser's specialty. She uses objects that have developed a patina over time and incorporates old beams or antique mantels.

Glasser was compelled to buy the house by the step-down living room and its beamed ceiling; these features reminded her of Spanish Colonial architecture, even though the style is actually Georgian Revival. A silver gilt French chandelier dominates the room. "I remember staying at a posada in Antigua, Guatemala," Glasser says, "and it being lit entirely by candles; there was no electrical lighting. It was incredibly beautiful, and ever since, I have tried to use more and more candles for the atmosphere they create at night, especially outside." The half-dozen antique mirrors in the living room reflect the candlelight beautifully at night and add to the airiness of the room during the day. "It's a little unorthodox to have so many mirrors in one room, but I love the glittering reflections."

From early on, Glasser introduced religious art into her home and made an effort to keep it looking light. While still in her twenties she purchased the pair of Italian gessoed putti, which now hang on either side of the fireplace in the living room. "I've had this passion for Spanish Colonial and Mission art for a long time. Having grown up without this sort of art in West Texas, I don't know where it came from, but these pieces speak to me spiritually." Mixing in light-colored upholstery, antique Oushak carpets, and French and English antiques, she has created a hybridized French country environment.

PREVIOUS SPREAD:

Decorated in creams and corals, the living room creates a soothing atmosphere for this collection of art and antiques. An antique English screen with a foliate pattern painted on canvas obscures the stairway. The large silver-leaf chandelier is lit with candles for parties and at Christmastime.

OPPOSITE:

ABOVE LEFT: A painting of the Virgin and child encircled with roses came from a South American estate.

ABOVE RIGHT: The face of this fruitwood santo, which is in the living room, is particularly expressive.

BELOW RIGHT: The master bedroom continues the restful palette while incorporating an eclectic mix of furniture and artworks. Above the eighteenth-century English Regency mantel is the painting of the Virgin from Guadalajara. Flanking the fireplace are two wing chairs; the wicker one to the left is American and the fully upholstered one to the right is an English Georgian version.

BELOW LEFT: Unframed tin retablos and other pieces of devotional art share shelf space with antique books in the library. On the bottom right is an English tobacco jar.

Illuminated by a bevy of candles, the coral library is frequently appropriated for intimate dinners. A Provençal boutis, or quilted bedspread, is used as a tablecloth. The tall santos are very dramatic standing in the deep recesses of the windows.

The library, with its walls of antique leather-bound books in glossy coral-colored bookshelves, offers Glasser another opportunity to indulge her love of candlelight. She frequently uses the space as an informal dining room, setting it aglow with lit altar candles in the corners and an eighteenth-century French parcel-gilt chandelier overhead. Discreetly placed on the shelves are antique retablos. "My favorite colors are coral and teal, and so many of these objects have those colors that they all work together very well," Glasser explains. Continuing the French country theme from the living room, she had the Italian dining chairs covered in an English version of a French toile, and the tablecloth is an antique Provençal boutis quilt.

The sitting area off the kitchen echoes the same decorative notes. Above the painted eighteenth-century French mantel is a Madonna and child painting that Glasser treasures for the roses painted along the edges and the coral-and-gilt frame. Serving as extra kitchen space, the twelve-foot-long Irish cupboard holds innumerable bowls and platters. "I look at it now and it looks like a mess!" Glasser notes. "But I do use them all." The coral-colored upholstered furniture is gathered on top of a rare floral-patterned antique Heriz carpet. Coral-and-cream toile curtains hang from iron rods, adding to the Provençal aspect of the room. As with the rest of the house, there is an unexpected affinity of color and texture between the spiritual objects Glasser collects and her varied antiques.

OPPOSITE:

ABOVE LEFT: Above the Portuguese coffer used as a dresser in the guest room hangs a Flemish mirror, one of three that Glasser bought for her first home. To either side are little torch-bearing angels called putti. Reflected in the mirror is a watercolor of anemones by Billy Goldsmith that Glasser's husband bought for her on their third date.

ABOVE RIGHT: A lifelike cherub with blue wings from Glasser's collection of angels.

BELOW RIGHT: Flowers and candles are found throughout the Glasser residence. A pair of gessoed angels flank another Flemish mirror above the fireplace.

BELOW LEFT: Just beyond the kitchen is this casual sitting area. The ceiling beams are antique and add character to the room. Among the antiques here is a round English cricket table next to the upholstered chair.

SAINTLY INSPIRATION

A superlative santo sets a European tone for a new dwelling

SANTA FE, NEW MEXICO

Having lived in London for a number of years, Gary and Barbara Aimes wanted to build a house in Santa Fe reminiscent of the historic homes they had visited in Europe, but within the local vernacular. Working with architect Sharon Woods they achieved a blend of pueblo style with a sense of history. The vigas, round hand-hewn timbers that support the ceiling in the living room, are from northern New Mexico, but were hand-adzed on-site. And the corbels were also carved on-site, using a French pattern. These traditional pueblo details and the thick plaster walls helped the Aimeses achieve their goal.

Central to the decoration of the house were several carved and painted images of saints, called santos, that the Aimeses purchased in Spain and Portugal. A santo from Guatemala, in a yellow dress with stylized flowers, commands attention in the living room. The Aimeses call her Our Lady of the Spa because of her earrings, painted nails and toenails, and flawless skin. "This was carved by a local artisan, not a schooled woodworker," says Barbara Aimes. "I have others that are more refined; she is more trunk-shaped and looks as if she were sculpted from a log. But I like her nonetheless." Aimes adds that the bright, almost primitive color of the saint's dress indicates that the santo is from the 1700s. The floral pattern on the gown reminds Aimes of the Provençal textiles she so admired during her travels in France.

PREVIOUS SPREAD:

Real hair, earrings, and the painted nails of this eighteenth-century Guatemalan santo led the Aimeses to nickname her Our Lady of the Spa.

OPPOSITE:

The santo stands on an antique Mexican mesquite wood kitchen table flanked by Moroccan melon-shaped lamps.

PALE WONDER

A neutral palette designed to enhance an extensive collection

PHOENIX, ARIZONA

A VERY PERSONAL COLLECTION of spiritual art dictated the design of this Phoenix home. The owner, a retired computer executive, bought the house new in 1997 and set about making changes to the structure that would integrate the art collection into its surroundings. Wooden floors were installed, mantels and vigas added, *nichos,* or niches, sculpted into the walls, and shelves built to hold specific santos and other religious articles. A thick coat of plaster made the house ready for its close-up as a stage set for an ever-growing collection.

The homeowner began collecting in the early 1990s, after visiting the gallery of Gloria List in Santa Fe. "I remember my first purchase perfectly well," she recounts. "We were having dinner at Gloria's and we were talking about all the santos she had around the house; they just fascinated me. I didn't really know she was a dealer, and it turned out her gallery was right next door. I left the party that evening with three santos!" And so a very erudite and passionate collector was born. More and more purchases ensued, and now every room in the house, down to the powder room, has at least one or two pieces of devotional art.

Each arched niche displays an antique bust of the Virgin above shelving holding a brilliant array of silver and vermeil objects on either side of the living room's Territorial-style fireplace. The most prevalent pieces here are the homeowner's collection of Mexican silver and vermeil crowns. These were not meant for people but rather as decoration for figures of saints and the Holy Family. Often sculptures of the baby Jesus feature him wearing a crown practically bigger than his head, as a sign of his importance. Halos, essentially crowns for holy figures, of different sorts are also prominent in this collection. There are the circular and almost platelike nimbuses, generally placed on the back of the head, and the halos that look more like tiaras, called *resplendors.* All these different types of headgear—which also appear in paintings—were created to bestow a glow to the figure, indicating the presence of a sacred being.

PREVIOUS SPREAD:

A pale gray background complements an extensive collection of devotional art. A nineteenth-century Mexican Saint Anthony with a period silver halo stands in the corner. Silver-gilded only on their fronts, the four early-nineteenth-century French cathedral candlesticks were never meant to be seen from behind.

OPPOSITE:

ABOVE LEFT: The built-in shelving flanking the living room fireplace holds gleaming metal liturgical objects, ex-votos, and reliquaries.

ABOVE RIGHT: Santos with articulated limbs like this eighteenth-century Guatemalan Virgin Mary are prized by the homeowner.

BELOW RIGHT: A life-size fully articulated nineteenth-century Saint Michael with tin wings from Guatemala stands by the window in the dining room. Draped over his shoulders is an antique vestment traditionally worn by priests during mass.

BELOW LEFT: This eighteenth-century *Coronation of the Virgin* originates from the School of Cuzco. Below, on the French seventeenth-century trunk, is a Chilean Christ child.

"These pieces, especially the santos, have a resonance to me even though I am not Catholic," the homeowner explains. "When my partner first came over, he was surprised by them and asked if they didn't freak me out a bit. They don't. In fact I find them calming, and now he's used to them, too."

Over and over again the peaceful and serene expressions on the faces of the santos and the Holy Family, and in her collection of paintings and sculpture, draw her in. In the bedroom several santos stand guard, each on its own simple plaster bracket or on the step-down platform flanking the fireplace. Another personal aspect of this collection is the homeowner's preference for articulated sculptures. In order to make the santos appear more lifelike, the artisans made them with movable arms and sometimes even legs. The santos were then dressed

in the costume appropriate to the personage, not unlike a child's doll. "Something about the movement appeals to me," the homeowner says. "I shift them around, sometimes sitting, other times standing. It's a work in progress." According to her, a large percentage of her articulated santos seem to have originated in Guatemala.

In her efforts to give the house a more historic atmosphere, the homeowner added several antiques. In the kitchen, for example, a nineteenth-century provincial French hutch shows off her china to its best advantage. Atop the hutch is an English sterling silver church service dated 1858. The set includes a pierced tray, an ewer to hold the water, two chalices for the wine, and two patens, which were used to hold the bread at the ceremony of the eucharist. Hanging from the hutch is a nineteenth-century polychrome angel carved in the sixteenth-century style. In the foyer, another antique tells an Old Testament story: the parable of Abraham and Isaac is depicted in carvings on the front of a late-seventeenth-century French trunk. Early nineteenth-century Russian icons sit on a wooden desk of the same period, from the Pyrenees, used as a nightstand in the master bedroom. A pair of brilliant blue Mexican angels genuflecting on a carved cloud, another of the homeowner's early purchases, balance the two sides of the bedroom with a jolt of color.

Refining and learning more about her collection of antiques and devotional art has become a passion for this collector. "Now when I visit Gloria's home and see a piece I like," she says, "I think, darn, she beat me to it!"

OPPOSITE:

ABOVE LEFT: Above the four-poster bed hangs an eighteenth-century School of Cuzco painting of the Virgin and child with lambs and cherubs.

ABOVE RIGHT: One of a pair of nineteenth-century Mexican angels kneeling on a sculpted cloud. On the early-nineteenth-century Pyrenean desk is an eighteenth-century Niño, or Christ child figure, sitting on a period chair.

BELOW RIGHT: The shelf supports on the wall of the master bedroom were built especially for these santos. To the right of the fireplace is one of a pair of eighteenth-century silver repoussé carta glorias, or altar card stands, from South America that have been converted into candlesticks.

BELOW LEFT: A Guatemalan articulated santo with a rosary around her neck.

COUNTRY STYLE

A Texan zinnia patch of a cottage and British sophistication in the city for an accessories designer

NEW YORK, NEW YORK, AND DALLAS, TEXAS

Cece Cord might be a society fixture and a designer of luxury accessories, but at heart she's a country girl with a Texas drawl. In a sprawling apartment in Manhattan and a cozy cottage in Dallas, Cord lives a life of casual comfort and finds refuge from her busy life. Greg Jordan, the late interior designer known for his chic yet traditional style, worked on both of Cord's properties, imbuing them with the larger-than-life personality of his client. Cord's collections of crosses and crucifixes, which she has been amassing since childhood, fill mantels and tabletops in both locations. "I started having this fascination with them when I was a girl," Cord explains. "My godparents gave me a little silver trunk with a silver cross inside for my Confirmation. Ever since, I've been hooked."

"This apartment has a country feeling right in the middle of Manhattan," Cord says of her New York place. "That's what I love so much about it. I've had it for about thirty-three years, and Greg redid it twice." An amalgam of furniture, art, and objects dear to Cord fill the rooms of this English country house transported to Midtown. Jordan first worked on this apartment at the beginning of his career. To hear Cord describe the experience, there were some early growing pains, but the two quickly became close friends. The current incarnation freshened up the aesthetic while maintaining the cozy feel that Cord so enjoys. She and Jordan dispensed with a formal antique oriental carpet in the living room and replaced it with sisal, and the walls were papered in a cream-and-beige stripe to create a more neutral environment for Cord's collections.

In the living room, English hunting dog paintings and the little antique dog chair beside the coffee table—a trunk, in this case—indicate Cord's love for dogs. Groups of crosses and crucifixes covering the mantel and side tables in the room offer a telling example of Cord's other collecting interest. To one side of the cut-velvet sofa, she has surrounded a favorite Russian cross mounted on a baroque base with family heirloom silver, making a particularly rich vignette. Another side table holds an odd little polychrome wooden cross with a ladder and spear on it—Instruments of the Passion. A still life by

PREVIOUS SPREAD:

A variety of textiles and red New Mexican chairs brighten the dining room, which is lit at night by the crosses with candles and vintage candlesticks.

OPPOSITE:

ABOVE LEFT: A cross and crucifix share space with a still life by Lady Sarah Stud. The walls in the New York apartment are wallpapered in a subtle beige and cream stripe.

ABOVE RIGHT: A pair of folk art votive holders illuminate a New Mexican retablo on the dining room/study mantel.

BELOW RIGHT: The living room is a gallery for Cord's collection of dog paintings. The wide front of the little chair next to the trunk indicates that it was made for dogs.

BELOW LEFT: A layer of devotional art freshens Cord's English country-house apartment. Here in the master bedroom, watercolors of birds and fowl, hung cheek by jowl, form a background to a collection of crosses, santos, and votives.

Cord's friend Lady Sarah Stud rests against it and the base of a crucifix. "I love the shapes of these crosses," Cord explains. "I appreciate the purity of the form."

Cord uses her study as a dining room, pulling up an English gateleg table to the camelback sofa and using simple green leather Queen Anne chairs for extra seating. A dozen or so primitive crosses, mostly from Ecuador, decorate the mantel under the large Audubon print Cord brought from her childhood home. Cord's collection of crosses shows the variety that can be found in this most common Christian image. Two sticks tied together form one; another stands out because of its red coloring; yet another has a Christ figure with a seldom-seen gilt *resplendor,* or halo, on His head; His cross and loincloth are painted in matching green. Amid all of these crosses a naïve New Mexican retablo's doors open, revealing a painted Nativity scene. Cord especially likes the antique New Mexican parade saddles on either side of the fireplace. "They have their original red-and-white saddle blankets," she says, "and they have silver pistols for bits!"

The master bedroom, with its buttercup-yellow glazed walls, displays more of Cord's eclectic mix of personal treasures. Another collection of crosses holds court on the mantel, along with a pair of repoussé silver candlesticks under a suite of eight watercolors of birds. The English country house theme is again enhanced here, with devotional objects that remind Cord of her Texas childhood. To the right of the fireplace, on an antique inlaid-wood English dresser, three crucifixes, a retablo of the Virgin and child encircled with a rose garland on a tall stand, and a pair of ornate Portuguese silver candlesticks practically obscure a small Georges Braque still life on the wall.

An array of crucifixes and silver candelabra on a George III dresser practically obscures the Georges Braque still life that hangs on the wall. The metal retablo to the left is on a stand surmounted by a cross.

"Everything has a special meaning to me in this house," Cord says of her Dallas home. "It all makes me smile. Not the least of which is Greg's decorating and transformation of it into, as he said, 'A sunny zinnia patch of a cottage!'" Cord's love of the southwest shines through in every room of this house, which she was inspired to buy twenty years ago just for the masses of wisteria climbing the front porch. Cord called in Greg Jordan a few years later to make sense of her accumulation of southwestern art and castoff family furniture. She recalls buying only a few Mexican tables; even the tortoise bamboo shades came from her first post-college apartment.

"Greg and I had such a fun time putting this house together, and I think that happiness shows," she says. "I like a more subdued color palette, but Greg convinced me to go with these brights, which just make me smile." Jordan used color boldly, to organize a group of objects or to highlight the sculptural qualities of the furniture. In the living room, for example, a collection of turquoise crosses stands on a table, and a pair of chairs gain visual prominence from their solid-colored upholstery. Pale yellow walls and similar window treatments throughout the house help tie its rooms together.

Crosses and crucifixes appear on almost every surface. On the dining room table, crosses function as candlesticks and a large one hangs on the wall with a pillar candle at its center. An assemblage of crosses and a retablo echoes a similar grouping in Cord's New York apartment, minus the Braque. More crosses, mixed with family photos, show up in Cord's bedroom, which features her childhood four-poster bed—its frame now stripped after many different paint jobs—piled with quilts and blankets. "There are so many crosses," Cord says, "that when my daughter was a teenager she asked me to remove them from the windows because the neighbors could see them and might think we were strange!"

Holding so many memories for Cord—from her great-aunt Anne's back porch rattan furniture to the southwestern memorabilia and devotional objects—this house serves as a place to recharge. "Most people go to a spa for a week," Cord says. "I can come here for two days just to fiddle around and come out happy."

OPPOSITE:

ABOVE: In the far corner of the living room, several turquoise crosses are displayed on a turquoise painted table from New Mexico, one of the few pieces of furniture that Cord bought for the house.

BELOW RIGHT: Featuring the Virgin Mary, this retablo is one of Cord's favorites because of the detail and bright coloration.

BELOW LEFT: Family castoffs, such as this Victorian parlor chair reupholstered in cowhide, appear throughout the house. Cord has collected crosses such as these since she was a young girl.

PAST PRESENT

Fashionable interiors designed for a collection of worldly objects

SARASOTA, FLORIDA

These days, the worlds of fashion and interiors mingle so closely that it is no surprise that clothing designer Adrienne Vittadini has turned her hand to designing interiors. As she demonstrates in her Sarasota, Florida, house, the casual mix-and-match nature of her fashion works well in the home, too. Antique icons may hold pride of place in a bedroom while, at the same time, reproduction santos appear on a dining table dressed with a quilted bedspread. Vintage fabrics such as ikats and suzanis also fit into Vittadini's eclectic style, introducing an element of foreign cultures.

The library exemplifies Vittadini's sense of liberty within the constraints of a rather traditional home. On one wall hangs a large drawing of a Buddha on paper purchased from a dealer in Hong Kong. Above the sofa, a coat purchased in Uzbekistan many years ago is framed in Plexiglas, while a suzani bedspread covers the sofa seat cushions. "The coat inspired a whole collection of mine when I was in fashion," Vittadini states. "I love the colors and patterns of all these tribal cultures." The term *suzani,* meaning "needlework," is associated with the traditional silken embroideries of Uzbekistan. In the nineteenth century, prayer mats, bedspreads, and other household items that were part of a young woman's dowry were embroidered using the suzani technique. During her post-college travels in the early seventies, Vittadini collected ikats, Balinese textiles woven using a resist-dyeing method that makes patterns appear as the fabric is created. Many of the objects in her home, including the

Bessarabian rug in the library, remind Vittadini of her childhood. "Before we left Hungary in 1956, during the failed revolution, my father taught me a bit about icons and rugs, and now having these objects around is very comforting to me."

Several icons in Vittadini's home adhere to traditional type, with their embossed silver covers and dark images of the saints or Holy Family. Icons in the Russian Orthodox Church work in much the same way as santos do for Roman Catholics, as representations that can be worshipped or that serve as a reminder of a saintly life. A pair of small icons in a double frame and a larger one on

PREVIOUS SPREAD:
Eighteenth- and nineteenth-century etchings from Parma hang above the headboard in a guest bedroom. The small cross to the left, said to be Transylvanian, was purchased in a Budapest flea market.

OPPOSITE:
ABOVE LEFT: A large floral painting from the fifties sets the color scheme for this dining room, which features an antique crystal chandelier, a gift from Vittadini's mother-in-law.
ABOVE RIGHT: An unframed icon depicts Christ as a richly dressed priest.
BELOW RIGHT: Decorating the dining table are reproduction santos from Brussels. The dinnerware is from Ceramica d'Este, which has a library of patterns dating back to the seventeenth century.
BELOW LEFT: These three nineteenth-century icons have a czarist provenance. The double one was probably meant for traveling.

a guest room nightstand have a czarist provenance. Another icon, which Vittadini acquired in Budapest, depicts Christ as an Orthodox priest, with richly embroidered garments and a bejeweled crown. "I had an early attachment to icons," Vittadini explains. "They anchored my youth, which was marked by leaving my homeland." Now Vittadini lives happily amid memories of her two previous lives.

Antique books and objects fill the shelves of Vittadini's cream-colored library. Brilliant red accents add drama to the room. The suzani embroidered coat is from Uzbekistan and was purchased as inspiration for a clothing collection Vittadini designed. A Chinese red lacquer table centers the room with an antique Bessarabarian rug underneath. To the right, a large Buddha drawn on paper was purchased from a dealer in Hong Kong.

CALIFORNIA VILLA

Evoking the ancient world with a contemporary spin

A HOUSE CAN BE SAID to be simply a sum of its parts, but in the case of the Montecito, California, residence that interior designer John F. Saladino shares with his wife, Betty Barrett, the mood and atmosphere they have created speaks volumes. The stone-walled home relates to its midstate location with an outdoor entry gallery, for example, and its lush gardens planted with agaves and palm trees. Positive comparisons to an Italian villa aren't mistaken, as Saladino's elegant architectural and decorative work have repeatedly referenced classical Greek and Roman history throughout his professional career.

In the transition from the motor court to the main foyer, the rustic beauty of the structure is immediately apparent. This indoor/outdoor space, a theme so typical in California, is fully furnished, but with an eye to the elements, as Saladino points out. "The table in the entry gallery is probably a nineteenth-century stage set piece. It is wooden, but the decorations on the front are sculpted from metal." Saladino regards this trompe l'oeil effect without concern as it makes for a sturdy piece that can withstand inclement weather. He continues: "And the lamp is made from an eighteenth-century Italian marble urn. It's heavy, so the winds won't knock it over and the shade is plastic in case it gets wet." Saladino's mother gave him the small statue of Saint Francis of Assisi on the table when he was a young man.

Inside, the entry foyer greets the visitor with a bit of local history. In one corner stands a carved French statue of Saint Barbara from about 1450. Saint Barbara, the patron saint of neighboring city Santa Barbara, also happens to be the patron saint of architects and builders

PREVIOUS SPREAD:

Deep stone window recesses provide an intimate space for small-scale antiques. Two Italian effigies, one seventeenth-century ivory and the other an eighteenth-century wood version, mingle with first-century B.C. Roman unguent jars for perfumes or precious oils.

OPPOSITE:

ABOVE LEFT: Saladino's mother gave him the small figure of Saint Francis of Assisi when he was a young man.

ABOVE RIGHT: The entry gallery is a protected, open-air space from the motor court to the main foyer.

BELOW: In the antiques-filled entrance foyer, a hand-blocked Fortuny textile with a velvet border contrasts with the stone walls. By the door, a small circa-1650 cabinet beneath the seventeenth-century Italian octagonal mirror holds a portrait of Saint Barbara and a seventeenth-century candlestick converted into a lamp.

FOLLOWING SPREAD:

LEFT PAGE: The Italian-style secret garden has a pair of neoclassical iron urns mounted on stone piers.

RIGHT PAGE, ABOVE LEFT: A stone Buddha sits in the agave garden.

RIGHT PAGE, ABOVE RIGHT: This cross-shaped reliquary hangs from a rope of black pearls.

RIGHT PAGE, BELOW: Stone walls are found throughout the house, including the ladies' bedroom. Above the fireplace is an early reliquary with a papal seal on the reverse.

among many other patronages. Legend has it that in the third century she was imprisoned in a tower by her father for disobedience. While there she converted to Catholicism, and her father denounced her to the local authorities, who ordered her death. Reportedly, lightning immediately struck and killed her father. The mere happenstance of her imprisonment in a tower led to her association with many of the construction trades. A slightly earlier image of Saint Barbara, from fourteenth-century northern Italy, shows her with a castle in the background. "Word gets out that I'm collecting images of Saint Barbara," explains Saladino of his growing collection, "and before you know it, all sorts of people are sending me leads or pictures of antiques related to her." An etching and an early photogravure depicting local scenes suggesting the home's locale are also here. The drawing is a British fantasy of what the native Californian population looked like. Under a candle sconce hangs an image of an unpaved State Street in 1850, a very early look at what was to become the city of Santa Barbara.

The 1929 house features a drawing room with a massive stone fireplace. The sofas are of Saladino's own design. The stripped-down space allows for the layering of a great variety of antiques, such as a pair of red velvet Louis XIII chairs and the small Napoleonic chair near the hearth.

"I had to have been a little nuts!" claims Saladino, explaining the history of the house. "It was built in 1929, but I bought it as a ruin. All new mechanicals were installed, new roofs, everything was put back into this shell of a house over a five year period." Having saved the house from the brink of collapse, Saladino went on to decorate it with his signature blend of modern upholstered pieces of his own design and a great mix of antiques. Scattered throughout, as in the entrance, are items of a devotional nature from many different cultures. A bookcase, for example, holds a Greco-Roman 200 B.C. Apollo statue; a Roman Empire–era Corinthian capital from Baalbek; and a little group of predynastic Egyptian terra-cotta figures called *ushabti,* meant to be servants for the deceased in the next world. This layered selection of objects is typical of Saladino's style, in which shiny and matte finishes balance each other, and modern and antique coexist naturally.

Upon close examination, it is easy to understand Saladino's attachment to the house. Not only are the large pieces carefully lit and displayed but the small, personal treasures have their own histories and are accorded respect. A gift to his wife on an important birthday, the reliquary that resembles a rosary hanging on the mantel, is a quiet highlight in her bedroom. At the bottom of the cross, a little hinged opening reveals a papal seal. The presence of the seal indicates that the relics contained within were considered legitimate by the pope. "The house is a vessel for all of the things I have collected," says Saladino. "You are looking at a lifetime of finding treasures."

OPPOSITE:

ABOVE LEFT: Soft-violet painted bookshelves hold not just books but antiquities and artworks. The capital on the top shelf is from Roman Baalbek (in present-day Lebanon), and the six terra-cottas on the lower shelf are pre-dynastic Egyptian sculptures, representing servants for the afterlife.

ABOVE RIGHT: A mid-fifteenth-century French statue of Saint Barbara. She is often associated with a tower; her father imprisoned her in one to discourage suitors.

BELOW RIGHT: As an ode to neighboring Santa Barbara, Saladino collects images of Saint Barbara as in this 1650 panel painting. Reflecting the garden just outside is a seventeenth-century Italian octagonal mirror; the lamp to the left is an electrified seventeenth-century candlestick.

BELOW LEFT: Ancient Egyptian figurines on an Italian walnut table.

Dozens of antique Italian and South American milagros have been applied by Gloria List to this nineteenth-century Mexican *trastero*; the chair beside it is from the 1920s.

SERENE LIVING

STAR SANCTUARY

A jewelry designer celebrates Zen living in the Hollywood Hills

LOS ANGELES, CALIFORNIA

In an aerie above Sunset Boulevard, jewelry designer Loree Rodkin lives in serene Asian splendor. This current incarnation of her home with Rodkin's precious Buddhas and Indian furniture is set in a sea of smoky topaz grasscloth walls and glistening mirrors with golden accents. Many of these objects decorated Rodkin's previous house, in the same neighborhood, but now gain from the twinkling lights and far-off vistas of her current home, an apartment she combined from two separate units with Panavision views over Los Angeles. Rodkin's visitors know they are in Hollywood, but a very distant, peaceful version of it.

This stage set is far removed from the one that made Rodkin famous in a previous career. As an interior designer for celebrity clients, she was known for velvets and brocades—a Goth-meets-Victorian blend with a heavy dose of Christian artifacts. She followed up that career with managing young up-and-coming stars, who appreciated her offbeat sensibility and single-minded determination, before turning to jewelry design.

PREVIOUS SPREAD:

The balcony with its antique Balinese Buddha and garden pots looks out over the Los Angeles skyline.

RIGHT:

The living room has been designed to create a clean-lined space. The neutral color of the upholstery highlights the cream goatskin rug and fur pillows without distracting from the view.

From a visual standpoint, Rodkin's jewelry and her home are complete opposites. Her creations in silver and gold are still rooted in medieval imagery, where they started off. Her home, on the other hand, is a glamorous version of Zen. Travels in Japan and Bali inspired Rodkin's change in decorating. "Prior to developing this style, my old house was so ornate it was torturing me," she says. "I needed something to clear my head. Designing detailed jewelry forced me to simplify my life in other ways, so I redecorated." Clearly, she went at it with her customary gusto.

Dispersed throughout the apartment that Rodkin designed, her collection of Buddhas sets the tone. Flanking a bank of curtainless windows in the living room, gilt Victorian pilasters support Thai Buddhas made of gilded wood. Aside from those Buddhas, the room relies on the

views for drama. It is essentially decorated in a palette of only gray and cream. The gray chenille upholstered pieces, which Rodkin's friend, interior designer Martyn Lawrence Bullard, had custom-made for her, sit atop a cream goatskin rug. "I tell my friends that I decorate in early drab," Rodkin jokes. "I am distracted by color, so it is easier for me to live without it." The light fixture above the dining table acts as a sculptural element in the apartment. Hung from a metal rod, three vintage rattan baskets from the 1960s that Rodkin illuminated are an ethnic take on a mod chandelier.

Black-and-white photographs by Brian English continue the Buddha theme and emphasize Rodkin's color palette. Running the length of the kitchen counter, four of English's images of Buddha rest on a shelf. A native Los Angeleno, English has worked with Herb Ritts, Horst P. Horst, Richard Avedon, and several other prominent photographers. As is witnessed in his photographs throughout the apartment, English shares Rodkin's interest in serene imagery.

Despite the unified color scheme and minimal furniture, the apartment does not appear monotonous. Several large, dramatic pieces punctuate the space and give it character. At the far end of the kitchen, against a mirrored wall, stands a five-foot-tall bronze reproduction of a Buddha's hand. In the living room, an oversize Balinese Buddha head carved from teak holds court between two antique Turkish lanterns mounted as sconces. "Although the Buddha appears to be broken," Rodkin explains, "it

OPPOSITE:

ABOVE LEFT: A Thai Buddha with mottled gilding sits cross-legged on a Victorian pilaster.

ABOVE RIGHT: Between two Turkish lanterns is a Balinese wood Buddha carved directly onto a broken tree trunk.

BELOW RIGHT: This gilded hand once belonged to a Chinese Buddha sculpture.

BELOW LEFT: Photographs of Buddha imagery by Brian English rest along a picture shelf in the kitchen.

is actually carved from one piece of teak that was found like this. I love the contrast between the finely carved face and the raw end of the log." Another lighting fixture, a capiz-shell triple chandelier by Verner Panton, acts as a floor-to-ceiling sculpture. Bullard selected the large triangular-shaped mirror in the living room. The elaborate piece, a filigree of gilded wood backed with crackled glass, is from a seventeenth-century Thai altar.

Rodkin's simple balcony now serves as her garden, with only an antique Balinese Buddha on a sculptor's trestle and bamboo stalks in a pair of antique Balinese pots—a far cry from her previous lush garden. But that's fine with Rodkin, who is pleased with her move. "This is a home to live in," she explains. "Here I am at peace. I have a small Manhattan apartment that is more of a closet to crash in at night. I'm always happy to come to this house."

OPPOSITE:

ABOVE LEFT: An intricate, seventeenth-century Indian door is the focal point of this hall.

ABOVE RIGHT: Reflected in a mirror is a Chinese Buddha hand resting on an African stool.

BELOW: Hollywood glamour meets Zen peace in Rodkin's master bedroom which is in keeping with the rest of the apartment. A seventeenth-century gold neckpiece from Bali hangs around an eighteenth-century Thai Quan Jin sculpture, a figure of great compassion.

DOUBLE VISION

*Transforming a home and pied-à-terre
into a calming space for Asian art*

NEW YORK, NEW YORK, AND SANTA FE, NEW MEXICO

"CHINESE CULTURE HAS ALWAYS APPEALED to me," says Linda Waterman, who first visited mainland China a year after Nixon's 1972 groundbreaking trip. "But I never owned a piece of Asian art until 2004." Now Waterman has two collections of predominantly Chinese pieces, one in New York City and the other in Santa Fe. In her New York apartment she features what she feels are the more sophisticated pieces, even though they may be thousands of years older than those in New Mexico. She started her collection in 2004, when she purchased a small Chinese jade and a "fat lady" pottery figure from the Tang dynasty (A.D. 618–907). Upon her return to New York, she took the pieces to Spencer Throckmorton, a noted dealer in Asian art, who was quite impressed with her acquisitions. "That visit gave me a confidence in my eye and encouraged me to continue my collecting," Waterman says.

Symbolic of good health and wealth, fat ladies date from the Tang empire, a period that saw the unification of vast territories and cultures in China. Waterman now has several. She points out one as particularly fine because of its pose and raised hand. These unglazed terra-cotta figures were modeled after period courtesans and, as Waterman notes, the plumper they are, the better, following the desired female shape of the period. Her smaller figures represent court attendants from the Tang dynasty and, along with the fat ladies, supposedly accompanied Chinese nobles in the afterlife.

Waterman's collection of jades dates primarily to the Neolithic period in China. Jade hair rings from the Liangzhu culture, makers of high-quality jade artifacts in the third millennium B.C., line several display shelves in the living room of Waterman's bright white apartment. "Like my home in Santa Fe, this apartment has undergone a sea change in style," Waterman explains. "What was my French salon has just now become a pristine space to display my treasures." Her other jade pieces are bi-discs, flat discs with central openings used in the ceremonial burial of the nobility during contemporaneous Hongshan and Liangzhu cultures in the north and southeast of China, respectively. With these ancient, Zen-like treasures freshly installed, Waterman is excited that this more peaceful period of her life is now reflected in her Manhattan apartment.

PREVIOUS SPREAD:

This display of Neolithic period jades includes several shelves of bi-discs, and the top shelf holds hair ornaments from the third millennium B.C. Liangzhu culture.

OPPOSITE:

ABOVE: Waterman's gallery-like New York City living room formerly resembled a French drawing room. As she began to collect Asian works of art, she transformed her home. Under several coats of gleaming white paint are traditional parquet floors.

BELOW RIGHT: Detail of a "fat lady" figure. The delicate painting gives her an even plumper appearance, which at the time of the Tang dynasty was a desirable trait.

BELOW LEFT: The Han dynasty warrior would have originally held armaments in his hands.

Whereas Asian artifacts are certainly seen more frequently in New York homes, it's not as much of a surprise to find Waterman's antique Asian artifacts in Santa Fe as one might think. The change from Western to Eastern art in her Santa Fe residence has been a gradual one but, without a doubt, all encompassing. For this former decorator it has been a huge transformation in her life. "My French and English antiques all were sold at auction, with the exception of a few pieces here and there," Waterman explains. "The needlepoint rugs were replaced with sisal, and the upholstery lightened up." The peaceful palette that has emerged allows the artworks from different cultures to happily coexist. Here in Santa Fe, Waterman has deployed her more rustic antiquities, which combine well with the plaster walls and white-painted vigas that support the ceiling of her John Gaw Meem–designed guesthouse. Meem is well known for both his pueblo revival architecture, which used tradtional pueblo building techniques, and his 1947 master plan of Santa Fe that led the way toward the city's preservation.

In Santa Fe, Waterman has her more rustic Asian antiquities, and a few folk art and Spanish Colonial pieces create an eclectic atmosphere. In this home, Waterman has redecorated in an effort to create a more neutral space for her burgeoning collection of Asian art.

Now, in place of a gilt mirror that used to reside above the fireplace, one finds a Khmer stone fragment of a lion from a Cambodian temple and three Han dynasty (206 B.C.–A.D. 220) figures from China. "I have always been attracted to natural and organic elements in my decorating," Waterman says. "These pieces have those qualities; they are quite primitive—not dressed-up animals—they have a purity that I seek." This certainly holds true in the display of Han ceramics, simple representations of soldiers and horses made for the tombs of aristocracy. These pieces reflected the deceased's social, religious, and economic standing and were also meant to accompany them in the afterlife.

Waterman's desire for tranquillity even extends to her contemporary art purchases. The large diptych in the living room is by Marcia Myers, a New Mexico artist. "I had been admiring her work for quite some time," Waterman recalls. "She mixes her own paints using Italian pigments and applies them using a frescolike technique. There is a worn, almost antique feeling in her painting that works so well here." Myers's painting picks up the muted tones of Waterman's Asian ceramics, and the top panel complements the oxidized bronze of a Chinese urn from the Warring States period (475–221 B.C.).

Since starting her Asian art collection, Waterman has been traveling throughout Asia regularly to study the different cultures and their artifacts. On many of these trips she travels with a friend who has been collecting for nearly twenty years. As she catches up to him in knowledge and in the breadth of her collection, the two have even started to purchase pieces jointly and share them now and then.

Amid a bright red lacquer box used as a side table and a Chinese armoire anchoring the far side of the living room, Waterman has made room for her Mexican coffee table with its whitewashed top and blue painted base. "I can't get rid of some of my Southwest folk art and Spanish Colonial pieces," she admits. Their sentimental value for her is apparent in the pieces decorating Waterman's dressing room. A brightly painted Crucifixion scene abounds with symbolism, from a burning bush to Veronica's veil, and tucked into the shelf support are photos of Waterman's three children. On another wall, a Mexican *trastero* storage cupboard contains a few Latin American pieces, ranging from a little Guatamalan niño to a charmingly ill-proportioned shepherdess and sheep from Mexico. Hanging above a diamond-paneled Spanish Colonial chest is a Madonna and child that Waterman bought off the back of a truck. "I saw it as the dealer was unloading his truck the night before a big flea market and I knew I just had to have it. I was there first thing the next morning. It's a rural Mexican piece done by a very talented artisan. I especially love the Jesus child; he has such a sweet face. It's one of the pieces from my old life that I just couldn't part with."

OPPOSITE:

ABOVE LEFT: A Tang horse with a removable saddle on top of a red lacquered Ming-style cabinet.

ABOVE RIGHT: This stone architectural fragment from the Cambodian Khmer period features a growling lion.

BELOW RIGHT: A Mexican painting of the Virgin and child hangs above a diamond-paneled Spanish Colonial chest.

BELOW LEFT: A contemporary Mexican folk art Crucifixion scene features a variety of Catholic symbols, such as the burning bush, Veronica's veil, and the die used to cast lots for Christ's garments.

GALLERY HOUSE

An antiques dealer gives stellar objects a chance
to shine in a historic home

SANTA FE, NEW MEXICO

"I SPEND ALL DAY IN MY GALLERY examining beautiful Spanish Colonial objects," says Santa Fe art dealer Gloria List. "And when I get home I just want to relax and have my house be as minimal as possible." While not exactly a temple to minimalism, List's adobe house nonetheless has an air of exacting placement that enhances the sculptural qualities of the interesting devotional objects she has collected over the years. Faced with the temptation of selling the things decorating her own home, she has concentrated on buying pieces for herself that she doesn't think will sell in her gallery. For example, a single gilded wing, probably from an angel statue, is mounted on a pedestal as an object to be admired. "That wing was purchased as a single piece, and most people want two. But for me, that there is only one doesn't take away from its beauty."

As for her decorating style, List tries to keep it as simple as possible. In the living room, windows are left curtainless, and the minimalist mantel on the fireplace she rebuilt fades into the stucco walls. List appreciates furniture made by designers whose work has a lasting quality. Soft, even light emanates from rice-paper Akira lanterns by Isamu Noguchi, the late Japanese American sculptor. Wood and stone tables made by Omer Claiborne, another Sante Fe dealer, and buttery-soft leather club chairs List has had for twenty-five years, from Thomas Callaway in Los Angeles, round out the comfortable space.

A pair of early-nineteenth-century santos from the Philippines depict Mary and Joseph. As with most of these figures, their hands and faces have been gessoed, but these were never painted, which is what appealed to List. "They have the most wonderful patina and creamy white coloration. Normally they would have been polychromed, dressed with clothes and wigs, but I found these as is. They are truly outstanding." A large headless eighteenth-century Mexican santo stands in the corner with milagros hanging from her neck. The silver milagros, or ex-votos, were traditionally offered in thanks to a saint for aid with an illness or for a realized wish. On another wall hangs a very rare altarpiece from Oaxaca,

PREVIOUS SPREAD:

Five silver repoussé Sacred Hearts are carefully hung above a linen slipcovered love seat in the sitting room. Sculptor Isamu Noguchi designed the Akira paper lamp and many others like it after World War II in an effort to revive the lantern-making industry in the Japanese town of Gifu.

OPPOSITE:

ABOVE LEFT: This articulated santo, which was meant to be clothed, is wrapped in gauze to substitute for the gown she originally wore.

ABOVE RIGHT: A silver repoussé Sacred Heart. The letters *GR* mean "grace received"; in this case, the Sacred Heart was offered by someone whose prayers had been answered.

BELOW: Turquoise pedestals supporting the cocktail table lend a jolt of color to the otherwise pale living room. The gown of the two-hundred-year-old Mexican headless santo in the far corner echoes the color.

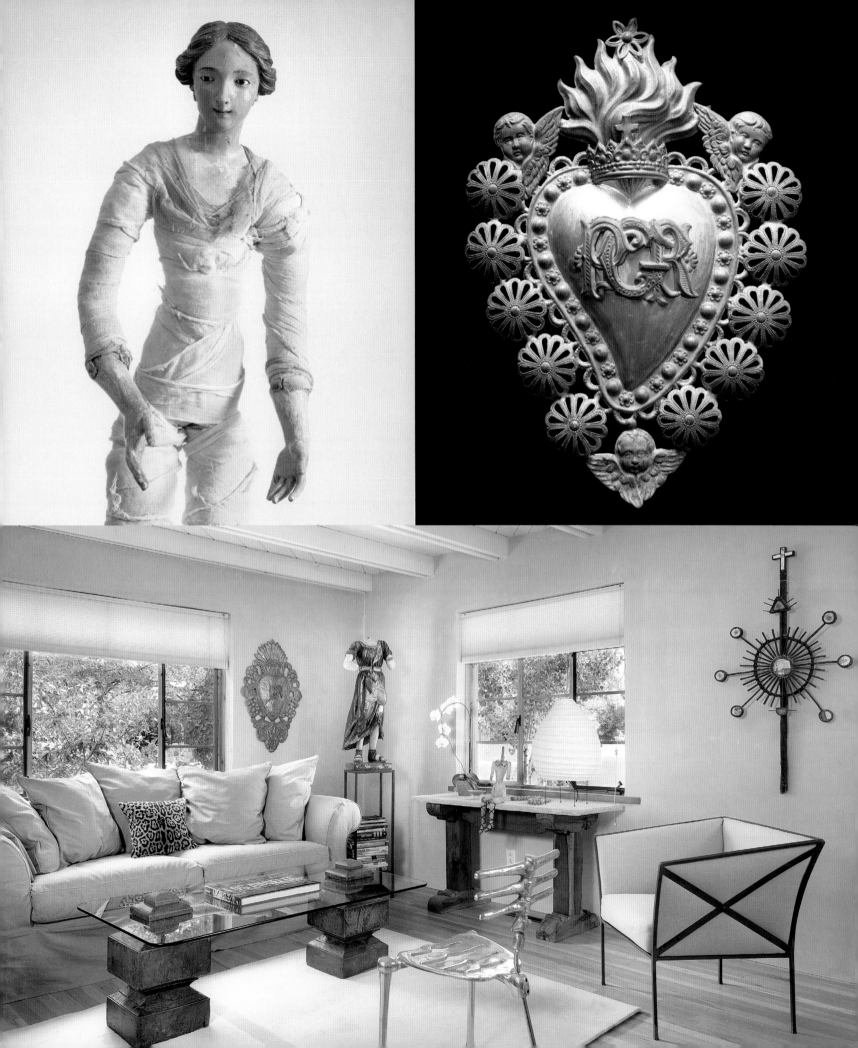

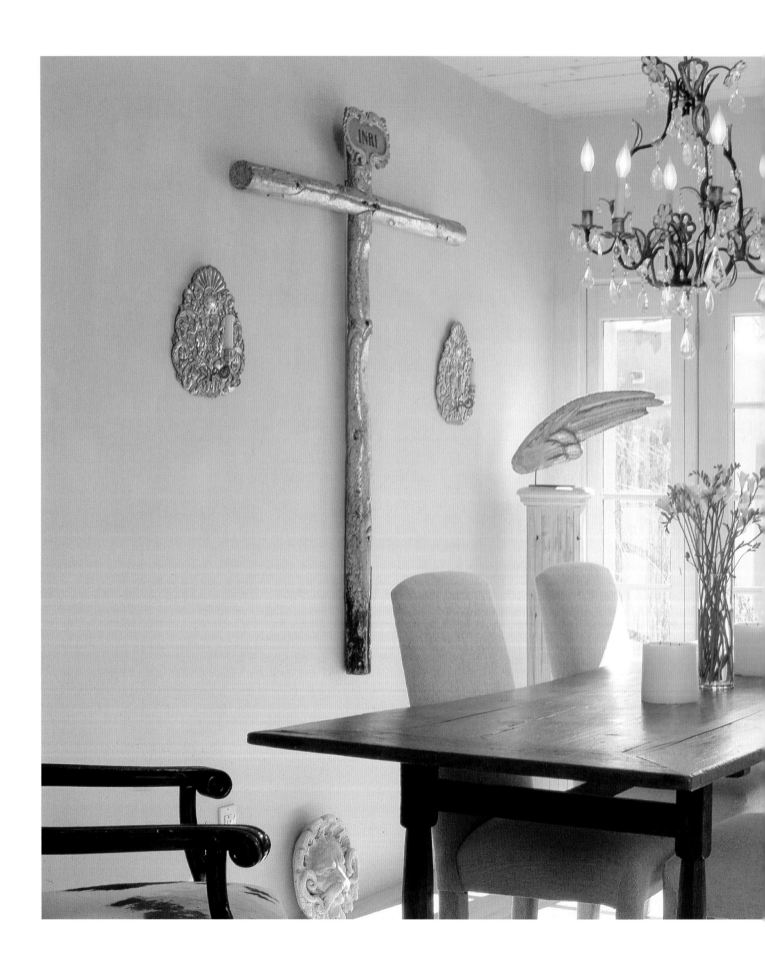

A Guatemalan silver- and gold-leaf cross is resplendent in the dining room. The wood is carved to look like actual branches with knots and bark. List says the silver repoussé Sacred Hearts from Bolivia are not particularly old, but new ones are still remarkably well made to this day. Above the French doors, a silver-leaf cloud that probably once supported an angel is from Venice.

Mexico, made of wood carved to look like twigs, with little mirrors on the ends and in the center. Some of the mirrors are painted with smiling suns, and List imagines that the center probably bore an image of the Holy Family that has since been lost.

In the dining room an Italian rock crystal chandelier is suspended above a French Provençal table surrounded by simple linen-covered dining chairs, and at both ends sit 1920s Spanish-style chairs that List had recovered in cowhide. One wall is hung with an array of silver Sacred Hearts bought in Parma, Italy, which have partially oxidized, just as List likes them. The Sacred Heart, which represents the heart of Christ with flames and a dagger wound and is always encircled with a crown of thorns, is meant to remind Catholics of their devotion to Christ. A stupendous five-foot-tall cross from Guate-

mala, made of silvered and gilded wood, dominates the opposite wall. Where the now-missing figure of Christ was nailed to the cross remain painted drops of blood.

As List describes it, her day-to-day business finding high-quality objects is getting harder and harder. "It used to be that people would come to me every week and offer me objects. Now I have to search them out, and it is more difficult to legally get good pieces out of South American countries, not to mention Italy, Spain, and France." For example, List points out the *trastero*, or Mexican storage cupboard, she bought in 1986, which is covered in little milagros that she used to buy for a dollar or two. "I couldn't do that now; they have gotten too expensive!" she claims. Still, as she says, when people come into her home or her gallery they feel as if it is a museum, with beautiful objects everywhere they look. "The artisans who made these milagros, santos, and other devotional objects may not have been famous or particularly well educated, but they put their soul and heart into these pieces, and it's still evident today."

Filipino early-nineteenth-century santos of Mary and Joseph stand atop the sculptural fireplace. They are simply gessoed and were never painted. Behind them a pair of Colonial Bolivian sterling silver angel's wings provide a decorative contrast. Also from Bolivia is the single eighteenth-century silver candlestick on a tripod base.

ART HISTORY

An erudite view of antiques in an elegant setting

SANTA FE, NEW MEXICO

For someone who never studied art history, Santa Fe antiques dealer Omer Claiborne has learned a lot on his feet. He knows Mexican linenfold carving and, more important, how it differs from the more ornate English linenfold of the Gothic period. He knows that pre-Columbian athletes wore yokes around the waist in a proto-basketball sport, but that his heavy version in stone was used only emblematically. Or that what looks like yet another cross is actually the last piece a nineteenth-century bricklayer would place on the top of a house to ward off evil spirits. "I never studied this art academically," Claiborne notes. "My only interest is aesthetic." That's only partially true, since he goes on to explain that once he has found an object that appeals to him, he likes to learn all he can about it and then put it up for sale.

Claiborne worked in Mexico City as an architect for many years, then, in 1980, he and his wife, Bunny, decided to settle in Santa Fe. Although he had collected pre-Columbian art in Mexico, he gave that up once he returned to the States. At first he imported Mexican art and antiques, but as the market became more saturated, he began traveling to other places that had similar art, such as Guatemala, Peru, and the Philippines. Over the years his gallery has gone through several incarnations, and now in semiretirement, Claiborne plans on keeping the one adjacent to his house. In 1997, he designed and built their present house, in the center of historic Santa Fe. Originally there was only one house, which Claiborne converted into his gallery. He then built a three-thousand-square-foot structure as their home. "It is traditional in that the windows have mullions and such," Claiborne explains, "but the interior has eleven-foot ceilings, and I don't like doors, so there are only two, one to the master suite and the other to the old house gallery space!"

The resulting large volume gives Claiborne's collection room to breathe and make an impact. Everywhere art is shown to its best advantage. In the hallway, for

PREVIOUS SPREAD:
A nineteenth-century Mexican table with linenfold skirting stands in front of the French doors at one end of the living room. The tall red and gilt candlesticks are removable from their bases, indicating that they were used for processions.

OPPOSITE:
ABOVE LEFT: An eighteenth-century figure of Christ stands atop a nineteenth-century cypress wood chest made in Mexico. The little silver baptismal shell and small documents box are also from the eighteenth century.

ABOVE RIGHT: This primitive painting of the Madonna and child from Peru is called a Mamacha. The Christ child is painted wearing a military uniform.

BELOW RIGHT: An early-eighteenth-century Mexican santo depicting either Saint John the Baptist or the Christ child.

BELOW LEFT: Above the fireplace in the master bedroom is a brick cross, which was traditionally placed on top of a house when the bricklayer had finished his job. A Sicilian jar in the form of a face sits on the mantel. Several different images are seen on the painting to the right, leading Claiborne to surmise that it was a sampler from an itinerant painter.

instance, with its French doors giving way to a court-yard, he has assembled objects that have a three-dimensional character, so they can be inspected more carefully. The console holds a nineteenth-century primitive Peruvian crucifix, notable for the star-shaped outline added to it. The piece includes many of the images related to the Crucifixion, ranging from Instruments of the Passion such as the ladder used to raise and lower Christ to the titulus inscribed with the Latin acronym *INRI*, which Roman soldiers are said to have nailed to the top of Christ's cross. The letters stand for Iesus Nazerenus Rex Iudaeorum, "Jesus the Nazarene, King of the Jews." A turned wooden candlestick next to the crucifix, also from nineteenth-century Peru, is interesting for its spiral carving.

Every piece in the Claibornes' house has a tale to tell. The open dining area in the main living space boasts an attractive paneled Mexican armoire. Claiborne's research into his ever-changing collection provides a rich background to his pieces. "This is different from a *trastero* in that it was meant to hold clothes," Claiborne says. "In the Colonial era, everything was folded and placed on shelves; there were no drawers except for the priest's

The dining room features a built-in display of primitive art from all over the world. The large Peruvian painting is a late-eighteenth- or early-nineteenth-century mythical figure of plenty from the School of Cuzco. The black pot to the right of the console is African, and the two candlesticks on the table are Colonial silver.

dresser in the sacristy and the occasional table that might have had a drawer." Several pottery jars from the sixteenth century sit on top of the piece. "These were originally used for wine and olive oil," Claiborne says. "The Spaniards protected their industries and exported these commodities throughout their empire, monopolizing the market—they are like the Coke bottles of their era!"

Then there are the rarities of Claiborne's collection, such as the seventeenth-century Mexican clay sculptures gracing the dining table. The raw clay figures look like artist's maquettes, or models, but were in fact probably just objects meant for a home altar. This group includes a candlestick with a handle, a vessel supported by a fleur-de-lys, and a figure on horseback that Claiborne concludes is Santiago, the saint thought to have conquered Mexico.

Of course, a number of pieces still hold mystery for Claiborne. A large dramatic portrait in the dining room defies analysis. "The painting is from late eighteenth- or early-nineteenth-century Peru," Claiborne says. "It is a large piece of some importance done by a South American Indian who was taught by a Spanish missionary. The woman depicted with a basket and jug most probably represents a mythical figure of plenty, but I'm still not sure." Claiborne has narrowed down the options regarding the nearby eighteenth-century Mexican figure of a child—it is either the Christ child or John the Baptist. "He's missing his arm," Claiborne says, "so I can't be certain of who it is! If he were holding a globe, it would be Christ, but if he were holding a cross, like a military standard, then he'd be John the Baptist." The guessing game isn't over for Claiborne; he enjoys the discovery and research too much, which ultimately benefits his clientele. One imagines he'll have his gallery for a long time because, as he says, "I'm afflicted with this disease called buying, so I have to sell!"

In the living room is a Mexican armoire with sixteenth-century Spanish jars for olive oil and wine on top. The painting is a Guatemalan retablo of the archangel Saint Michael, shown with wings and a sword. The frame, a good example of an eighteenth-century Spanish frame, is not original to the piece.

ASIAN PEACE

Asian-inspired modernity and a collection to match

NEW YORK, NEW YORK

In an increasingly hectic New York City, some collectors choose Asian art for its calming influence. For Steven Rockmore, a marketing consultant for residential developers, Asian artwork fits especially well in his apartment building from an aesthetic standpoint. Not only does Rockmore have a personal interest in Asian art, but twenty years ago, when his building was constructed, its Japanese investors hired him as a consultant. He suggested that the developers honor Japanese culture within the building's design. The courtyard was created as a Japanese garden, with a brook and a traditional teahouse, and the lobby features an antique Japanese screen. The garden courtyard was in fact so important to the overall scheme that Rockmore persuaded the developers to have the living rooms, rather than the bedrooms, face the garden so that residents could enjoy the view while they were awake.

"I've always liked Asian art and culture, and this building represents that with a Japanese viewpoint," Rockmore explains. "I collect artworks from other cultures, but they all coexist happily here." His collection is constantly evolving and always improving. Rockmore began with a few pieces he had inherited from his grandmother, including a jade figure of Confucius and some eighteenth- and nineteenth-century ceramics. Starting around 2000, Rockmore began collecting in earnest. "I realized that it was a field where it was still possible to get authentic pieces out of China and own them. They'll clamp down soon, so I am motivated to get art now.

I have pieces from the beginning of time to the thirteenth century." The constraints, he notes, are space and money. He doesn't buy just by the case but rather with an eye to getting better and better pieces.

"I am drawn to the larger pieces because, in this environment, they are so sculptural. There is something very contemporary about them. For example, the three Han dynasty figures standing between the windows are from the time of Christ, yet they are almost abstract." Rockmore cites his delicately carved Tang period marble Buddha as a restorative influence in his apartment. He has paired it with a very graphic print by Ellsworth Kelly, which doesn't compete with the serenity of the ancient sculpture. Other objects are just right for their spots,

PREVIOUS SPREAD:
Rockmore's first Asian antique purchase was this Tang horse that stands on the coffee table of his living room.

OPPOSITE:
ABOVE LEFT: A trio of Han dynasty pottery figures appeal to Rockmore for their abstract nature.
ABOVE RIGHT: A bronze figure from Burma and a celadon porcelain plate share space on the dining area buffet.
BELOW RIGHT: An Ellsworth Kelly print hangs over the inlaid sideboard. From left to right, the sculptures are a Tang dynasty "fat lady," a marble Tang dynasty Buddha, and a Han dynasty court figure.
BELOW LEFT: Han dynasty warriors on a living room windowsill overlook the verdant courtyard.

such as Rockmore's first purchase, a Tang horse that doesn't overwhelm the coffee table. Despite his interest in Chinese culture, he isn't too strict about collecting only Chinese artworks. A bronze figure from Burma watches over the dining area from a console, and the Thai jug from the Sukothai period is noteworthy for its pale green glaze and elegant proportions. With this eclectic mix of objects, Rockmore has created a peaceful oasis in the middle of the bustling city.

The spacious treetop-level living room includes a dining area. It is a serene space for Rockmore's collections of Asian art and contemporary paintings, such as the Marcia Myers piece on the right. On the dining table is a large sixteenth-century Sukothai pot with a pale jade-green glaze.

Twelve gold stars resemble a halo around the head of the Virgin Mary in a painting above the fireplace in the living room of Jane Smith's Colorado house.

HISTORIC SENSIBILITY

LANDMARK APPRECIATION

A renovation to bring balance back to a classic 1920s home

HOUSTON, TEXAS

DEVOTION TO THE HISTORIC CHARACTER of her Houston home led Pam Pierce to oversee its ten-year renovation. The result: an antique-filled home ready for its next hundred years. "We haven't worked on it constantly," Pierce qualifies. "But it was a bit more than the simple paint job I told my husband it would take when we bought the house! We are the seventh family to live here, and constant updates and repairs are necessary." Pierce clearly enjoys the challenges her house presents, and has created a home for her family that incorporates many of her own interests, including historic architecture, religious artifacts, and nonfussy decorating.

As an interior designer for more than thirty years, Pierce extols simplicity as her guiding principle, something she has been trying to teach her clients. Her Provençal-style living room is testament to her teaching. "I think that a home should provide respite from the outside world," she says. "You don't have to overdo it." Above the eighteenth-century living room mantel Pierce bought in Paris hangs a seventeenth-century wood carving that resembles a cross in its blocky silhouette. Across the mantel itself are architectural finials, a column capital, and several Venetian altar candlesticks in grays, whites, and faded golds. This neutral palette continues throughout the room. Pierce selected the same coarse heavyweight natural French linen to cover all of the furniture. Opposite the fireplace, drama comes from a large French Regency mirror and one of a pair of 1920s French chandeliers, with its original wooden candlesticks added for show.

"My husband bought me my very first santo, when we were first married," Pierce says. "There is a serenity they bring to a house that I think is important and goes back to my belief that a home is a sanctuary." A pair of large santos in the dining room make the point. One is a Madonna from Mexico; the other, a Saint Francis, a symbol of kindness to all creatures great and small. In the master bedroom, an eighteenth-century Italian walnut bureau holds a set of four santos depicting the evangelists

Matthew, Mark, Luke, and John. These four apostles of Christ wrote the first Gospels of the New Testament describing His life and death. The eighteenth-century figures were covered in many coats of paint when Pierce purchased them. She had them carefully stripped down to the layer of white gesso on the bodies, and their faces and hands were cleaned down to their original paint.

A true admirer of old homes, Pierce ensured that renovations to her 1926 house were in keeping with its age. "We live in a historic neighborhood of Houston, and I think it is important to preserve the character of the house," she says. "You can't just put in Sheetrock walls; you have to use plaster. Here we had to remove the seventies renovation, which wasn't very sensitive to the house,

and bring it back to its original state." To add even more age and history to her house, Pierce installed special architectural elements throughout. Reclaimed oak floors add character to the living room, with its arched windows and eighteenth-century French fireplace. A recent flood in the kitchen necessitated a thorough remodeling, which included replacing the floors with nineteenth-century cathedral marble flooring and installing new custom casement windows that fit with the rest of the house.

A combination of antiques, architectural salvage, and devotional artifacts have created a house that gives Pierce a peaceful break. She reached her goal over a long period of renovation, but living with the project made for fewer mistakes. As she peeled away the layers from previous owners, the house became hers. "I'm constantly busy at work," Pierce says. "This house is a relaxing refuge to me. When I get here at the end of the day, I just close the gate, and it is my universe. It is soothing and replenishes me."

OPPOSITE:

ABOVE: Seating in the dining room is rather unorthodox; on one side of the eighteenth-century walnut trestle table is an upholstered bench, matched on the other side by an eighteenth-century Swedish Queen Anne triple-back settee. Below the contemporary painting by Hayes Friedman is an eighteenth-century Basque sideboard.

BELOW RIGHT: Santos of the four evangelists, Matthew, Mark, Luke, and John, stand on an eighteenth-century Italian walnut chest.

BELOW LEFT: The master bedroom continues the pale palette of the house with white linens and embroidered voile bed hangings. An eighteenth-century Portuguese Colonial table serves as a night table.

CABIN STYLE

A Colorado log cabin expands with a contemporary note

EMMA, COLORADO

Moving from the ruddy browns of New Mexico to the vibrant greens of Colorado has been a good change, says interior designer Jane Smith. She brought her santos, Navajo rugs, and Santa Clara pots with her from Santa Fe and integrated them flawlessly into her 120-year-old log cabin in Emma, Colorado. She applied her experience from years as a professional interior designer to the interiors, in the gut renovation of the cabin, and in the construction of a new addition.

"I worked with Gary Ferguson, a local architect, who lifted the cabin and put in a foundation where there had been none, stripped four layers of siding off of the exterior, added a fireplace, and installed new floors," Smith explains, describing just part of what was done to update the cabin. "This cabin started off as a one-room house, and now I've turned that into my living room and added a small house around it." Throughout the process, the designer in her was trying to create spaces for her artworks and a flow between the old and the new. "It was important to be able to see the pieces in my collection with distance between them so they wouldn't appear crowded."

In bringing the house up-to-date, Smith introduced several contemporary pieces of furniture and objects that have a handmade quality to them. The living room, for example, feaures a pair of bright red stools by French furniture designer Christian Liaigre, and the luggage-tan leather and cream linen sofas are of her own design. Upstairs in the guest bedroom, the bed and bench, hand-crafted of woven leather, were designed by Henry Beguelin, who is perhaps better known for his leather fashions and accessories. The eclectic mix extends to the breakfast room, with its antique French marble-topped pastry table surrounded by Mario Bellini–inspired red leather chairs. "I love red," Smith says. "And the original Bellini chairs don't come in red. I bought these from Crate and Barrel!"

Carefully selected and placed paintings and objects animate the house. Crosses, in particular, hold special

PREVIOUS SPREAD: A santo in a vivid blue dress guards the vestibule to the master bedroom. The table and the mirror behind her are both Peruvian. Throughout the house, as here, the interior doors are antique Mexican.

OPPOSITE:

ABOVE LEFT: A standing seam metal roof, white fish-scale shingle, and a front porch in the new addition to the cabin create a Victorian farmhouse image.

ABOVE RIGHT: The antique Peruvian santo was purchased with the silver earrings; however, neither the flowers nor the ribbon with the ex-voto are original to the piece.

BELOW RIGHT: Planted in a Mexican stone baptismal font, red impatiens greet visitors to Smith's home.

BELOW LEFT: A marble Christ figure on a museum mount in the master bedroom. This sculpture may have been part of a Nativity set, where it would have rested in the manger.

The one-room log cabin has been turned into the living room. Smith
added the fireplace. A 1920s Navajo rug sets the room's palette.

meaning for Smith. She finds them to be her personal peace symbol. From the nail-head trim on a stool to the simple cross woven into a Navajo rug to the enormous cross in the bedroom, examples abound. Notably, most of them are not crucifixes, thereby emphasizing their geometric appeal as opposed to their otherwise religious connotations. "So many people ask if I'm really religious," Smith comments. "But I simply find these objects beautiful in their own right, and in some cases have superimposed my beliefs on to them." Such is the case with a small bronze figure of the crucified Christ with female breasts. In Smith's opinion, it is not heretical or blasphemous; for her, the little sculpture is a liberating image indicating that even a woman could be the savior of the world.

Smith strove to combine old and new in the architecture of the house, the furnishings, and the artworks in order to create a harmonious whole that blurs the line between rustic and modern. In bringing the cabin up-to-date, the log walls were cornmealed, a gentler form of sandblasting, which preserved much of their patina. And the four-hundred-year-old oak plank floors and antique Mexican doors, with their original paint, are also integral to creating a relaxed environment that doesn't compete with Smith's art, antique or contemporary. From the garden, which features an antique baptismal font used as a planter, to the Civil War–era Union flag in the front hall, this eclectic array of antique decorative elements brings a sense of history to a carefully restored and expanded building.

An Italian mirror in the front hall reflects a painting of the Virgin Mary in the living room. On the gilded shelf bracket stands an antique cross painted with the Instruments of the Passion and a santo holding a rosary that Smith placed around his neck.

GALLERY LIFE

Southwestern arts on display in a nineteenth-century pueblo house

SANTA FE, NEW MEXICO

GALLERIST NEDRA MATTEUCCI LOVES all things southwestern, so it's no surprise that her house is a compendium of the last five centuries of art found in the area. Her Territorial house, built in 1860 for Mexican general Juan José Prada, and the eighteenth-century pueblo-style guesthouse, serve as a spacious and atmospheric backdrop to her collection. Operating three Santa Fe galleries taught Matteucci a great deal about the arts and antiquities of the area. One gallery specializes in early Taos painters, another in Native American antiquities, and a third in contemporary artists working in a traditional manner. And although Matteucci doesn't deal in devotional art, she is a collector of it, commenting, "I just happen to like it as an art form."

At the entrance to Matteucci's house visitors are greeted by a seventeenth-century Mexican Virgin of Guadalupe painted on copper. It is a brilliant image of the Virgin encircled in golden rays, with a choir of angels holding crowns and a series of smaller images depicting the story of the Visitation of the Virgin at Guadaloupe. Further on, a resplendent Mexican Empire altar from the eighteenth century, which Matteucci has repurposed into a console, grabs one's attention. The heavily gilded piece supports two santos: a Spanish Colonial Saint Anthony of Padua and a Mexican Saint Peter that has been turned into a lamp.

"The den has artworks which are more representative of my galleries," Matteucci says. There one finds a particularly fine 1932 landscape by E. Martin Hennings, a leading member of the Taos Society of Artists, a small artists' colony that exhibited together from 1915 to 1927. The oil painting hangs over an eighteenth-century Mexican credenza made of sabino wood, a particularly hard cypress wood that is now protected by law in Mexico. On top of this elegantly paneled piece sits another Mexican santo that has been turned into a lamp and a valuable 1920s Santa Clara polished Blackware pot. Made using a traditional coiling method and buffed to a gloss with polishing stones, the pot is by Sara Fina Tafoya, the mother of Margaret Tafoya, who popularized Santa Clara pottery.

Mixing her religious art with nondevotional artworks by local artists, Matteucci has created an elegant home that celebrates the rich cultural heritage of the area.

PREVIOUS SPREAD:

A Spanish Colonial screen sets the stage in this corner of the house. The elaborate Mexican Empire gilded altar is from the eighteenth century. The santo on the credenza is a Spanish version of Saint Anthony of Padua.

OPPOSITE:

A seventeenth-century Mexican Virgin of Guadalupe painted on copper greets visitors in Matteucci's foyer.

MONASTIC LAIR

Medieval and Renaissance art and antiques high above the Hudson

NEW YORK, NEW YORK

High above the Hudson River on Manhattan's West Side, a classic 1920s apartment holds a surprising array of European Gothic and Renaissance furniture and art. Adding a smattering of pieces from other cultures, the couple who resides here designed their home around their ever-growing collection. Modern furniture doesn't really have a place in this home; even the bed is of Italian or possibly Spanish Renaissance era, and has a provenance from the William Randolph Hearst collection. "I first started collecting at a tag sale years ago, when I bought a seventeenth-century walnut coffee table," the husband explains. "It wasn't truly authentic in that it had been put together from other antiques, but that sparked the interest." Many pieces from the period have similar issues regarding their authenticity; however, the couple researched and studied the field thoroughly to ensure the quality and merit of their artworks. One of their prized possessions is a circa-1180 wooden Madonna from a Cologne, Germany, workshop; they know of only two other similar existing examples. "That sculpture is exquisite. It exemplifies the turn from Romanesque to Gothic carving. It is probably our most precious object." Another favorite is the desk in the study, from seventeenth-century Spain, a completely original, significant piece in lustrous dark brown walnut, with iron stretchers in the shape of a trident. "This furniture is undervalued in today's market. Most people find it clunky. We've purchased much of our furniture and objects at country markets, where there was little or no appreciation for it."

The pieces of furniture in the apartment represent a conglomeration of Gothic through Renaissance design. A Spanish *papelero,* a multi-drawer traveling secretary, with gilt and paint decoration and bone inlays, shows Moorish influences that still existed in Spanish arts of the seventeenth century. In the dining room, lit with a sixteenth-century Flemish bronze chandelier, an unaltered Umbrian credenza stands to one side, holding

PREVIOUS SPREAD:

In the corner of the dining room, a seventeenth-century Thai Buddha head from the Stanley Marcus collection is an imposing presence. The ceramics are seventeenth-century Persian Kubachi ware. An African Baule sculpture from the Ivory Coast is on the credenza; it represents an ancestor who was revered and honored.

OPPOSITE:

ABOVE LEFT: A very rare sixteenth-century majolica plate from Lyons depicting the Last Supper.

ABOVE RIGHT: An Italian Baroque gilt-wood mirror is the backdrop to an assortment of Asian decorative elements and a pre-Angkor Cambodian Vishnu from the seventh century.

BELOW RIGHT: A lustered Italian majolica plate depicting Saint John the Baptist, circa 1520.

BELOW LEFT: On the carved bracket is a late-Gothic sculpture of the Madonna by Tilman Riemenschneider, a German sculptor. Now electrified, the silver candlesticks to either side of the desk from Estremadura, Spain, were made in South America but based on an Italian design.

candlesticks and a majolica plate. Although simple in design, the leaf garland brackets at each corner give the credenza a quiet beauty. The rather stern sixteenth- and seventeenth-century fratello chairs in the bedroom are another classic example of furniture of this period. With their original embossed-leather seat and back rest, the chairs were meant for use by monks in a monastery.

As the couple acquired furniture, then began adding sculptures, they found their home full, so they turned their acquisitions budget to decorative accessories. European and Persian ceramics from the fourteenth through seventeenth centuries find pride of place in the dining room, on either side of the gilded Spanish mirror. Three seventeenth-century Kubachi plates from Persia contrast with an oversize Thai Buddha head from the same period. Kubachi wares were produced during the Safavid dynasty (1501–1722), which saw a return to traditional pottery-making for the first time since Mongol invaders destroyed the centers of ceramic production. A time of innovation in the craft, this period saw the introduction of a blue-and-white palette that corresponded to the early Chinese Ming dynasty, and a polychrome painted style. Four fourteenth- and fifteenth-century examples of Hispano-Moresque pottery hang on the

A broad array of antiques fills the living room of this Manhattan apartment overlooking the Hudson River. To the left is a seventeenth-century octagonal center hall table with Flemish chairs; the altar candlestick holder on it is Gothic.

other side of the mirror. This pottery with Islamic decorations, created in the south of Spain, marks the transition from Islam to Catholicism in Spain as the Catholic kings of Spain drove out the Muslims. In comparison, the wares of Renaissance-era Gubbio, in Italy, are squarely in the Catholic tradition, as in the majolica ware plate with a painting of Saint John the Baptist in its center. The artisans in the Umbrian town of Gubbio were the only ones

OPPOSITE:

ABOVE LEFT: In the master bedroom, a French or Flemish tempera-on-panel of the presentation at the temple has been reframed in a seventeenth-century Italian gilt-wood frame. The 1580 Venetian enthroned Madonna and child was originally a private devotional piece.

ABOVE RIGHT: The Hudson River and a nineteenth-century Turkish silk-velvet pillow cover form a backdrop to a fifteenth-century French statue of Saint Martha with a Tarasque on a chain. The Tarasque is the mythical beast—half fish, half dragon—that Saint Martha legendarily captured, saving the people of the Camargue.

BELOW RIGHT: Bone, gilding, and paint decorate this seventeenth-century Spanish *papelero,* or traveling desk. An early mid-Gothic, Nottingham alabaster is on the left, showing Saint Peter welcoming souls to heaven. Only two or three others are known to exist of this subject. In the middle is a classic figure from Gabon that was meant to guard the deceased. At right is a seventh-century Mon culture Thai Buddha head.

BELOW LEFT: Two versions of Saint Sebastian. In the arched panel painting, the saint is depicted with the Virgin Mary and Christ child. In the corner, the sculptural Saint Sebastian, circa 1480, is from southern Germany and is the height of late-Gothic sculpture.

with the secret to making lusterware, which involved the application of a metal oxide glaze that imparted a golden iridescence to the finished piece, rendering Gubbio's pottery even more coveted.

Aside from the European artworks found throughout the apartment, the couple also collects objects from Africa and Asia. "My wife's sister was living in Bangkok, and we visited a few times and developed a taste for pre-Khmer art from seventh- and eighth-century Cambodia, which is now getting a lot harder to collect." Flanked by a pair of Italian Baroque–inspired South American silver candlesticks, a collection of African ivory bracelets, pendants from Burkina-Faso, an Angkor Wat–period head, and a Cambodian torso sit on a desk from Estremadura, Spain. Another antique table displays a group of decorative Asian artifacts. Attesting to the couple's worldly interests, the collection includes an Indonesian pounder, a ceremonial African swirl headdress, and a seventh-century pre-Khmer Vishnu sculpture.

Combining artworks of many varied cultures hasn't been problematic for the residents here; as the husband explains, "Our interests have become complementary; and we have each learned a great deal from the other. And since practically all early art is devotional in nature it ties together in a rather abstract way."

PUEBLO BEAUTY

A historic compound brought back to life in El Zaguán

SANTA FE, NEW MEXICO

Nancy Lacy follows the sun. In the spring and fall she can be found close to her extended family in Indianapolis, Indiana; wintertime is spent in Scottsdale, Arizona; and she is devoted to the summertime skies of Santa Fe, New Mexico. Lacy started off her career as a psychologist, and after twenty years she left the field and became an interior designer. Now she finds herself back in psychology and working as a part-time designer. She purchased her first Santa Fe house in 1998 and spent two years restoring and decorating it, and just two years ago bought her second house, across the road, for use as guest quarters. She explains that she bought both houses sight unseen and that as long as the houses had good bones, she knew she could make them work.

The historically rich main house was originally part of El Zaguán, a large property first owned by James L. Johnson, a mid-nineteenth-century Santa Fe Trail merchant. Johnson built a substantial villa in what was then the edge of the city. Over the years the property changed hands, and in 1979 a private corporation transferred the land and buildings to Historic Santa Fe Foundation. The land now houses the foundation offices, exhibition space, and private apartments for visiting artists. Lacy's residence, one of four privately owned houses in the area, was originally a cowshed and then grew until, at one point, it became a house for farmhands and, finally, a private residence in the early 1900s.

"I have tried to restore the house to an earlier era," Lacy explains, "but at the same time making it totally functional for the twenty-first century." Her two-year renovation, full of custom details, brought the house back in time while making it work for her family's needs today. For example, the original brick floors are laid directly in the sand, without a foundation, in the traditional manner of pueblo houses, and the walls have been replastered with Structolite, a soft pink plaster. Every room has a fireplace, even the master bathroom, which used to be a bedroom. The wooden ceiling beams, called vigas, and the columns throughout the house were sandblasted to

PREVIOUS SPREAD:

The living room and dining area of this thoroughly restored pueblo house feature the original vigas on the ceiling and columns that have been sandblasted to bring back their original coloring. The chest, used as a coffee table in front of the sofa, is Spanish and originally stored a bride's dowry.

OPPOSITE:

ABOVE LEFT: A nineteenth-century Eastern European carved and painted Crucifixion scene rests on the mantel of the beehive fireplace in the corner of the living room.

ABOVE RIGHT: A large Russian icon of an evangelist looks over a heavily carved Irish desk and a William and Mary chair draped with a paisley shawl.

BELOW: Peruvian doors dating from the late 1800s have been set into the wall to the right of the fireplace, where they hide the television and stereo equipment. A traditional hand-punched pigskin shade tops the wrought-iron lamp at left.

Located across the street from the main house, the guest quarters are in a building that dates back to the 1930s, when it was a one-room structure. The decor here is similar to that of the main house, with antique doors used for built-ins and hand-plastered walls.

remove years of stain and varnish and to bring them back to their original appearance. The result: a light and airy house that seems as if it has always been that way.

When it came time to furnish the house, Lacy was well prepared with a warehouse full of furniture, accessories, and artworks she had been buying for years. "My husband would look at me and say, 'What are you going to do with that?' and now of course he's saying, 'Oh my gosh, she pulled it together!' You know, if you buy what you love, it will all come together beautifully." When Lacy was done with the painstaking renovation, she raided her storage spaces and put together a house that unfolds seamlessly. "I feel like these objects are old friends from two and three hundred years ago having a get-together in my house!" she says. There are art and antiques from all over the world. There are Russian Impressionist paintings, many antique Lithuanian sculptures and crosses, Mexican candelabras, French dressers, an Italian chandelier, and several pieces of Spanish furniture. The

eighteenth-century Italian secretary in the living room is from a clothing boutique Lacy used to frequent. "The shop was decorated to the hilt, and I wrote many a check on that desk for some beautiful clothes. When [the boutique] closed I knew I had to have [the secretary]."

The artisans Lacy met along the way came to her aid, adding another layer of authenticity and interest to her decorating project. Carpenters retrofitted the Indian grain chests into vanities for the master bathroom, and Jill Rounds, a Taos, New Mexico, tile maker, copied designs from the cabinets and crafted the matching tile backsplashes. Decorative throw pillows are made of pigskin stenciled in gold with Fortuny prints and some are also inset with antique textiles. Southwest punchwork designs in geometric patterns and crosses decorate a few of the pigskin lampshades. Antique doors that Lacy collected serve to cover the entertainment center she had built into the wall. The cross-shaped door pulls were purchased in Los Angeles many years earlier.

"The guesthouse is the fantasy home you always dream of as a child," Lacy comments. "And as an adult, it is the best way to have guests—across the street and in total comfort!" It is a charming space, with a slightly French country cottage look. Part of a small artist's colony, this house didn't have as many of the original details as the main house, so Lacy felt free to stray from the typical pueblo style. She had the brick floors mortared, for example, and tinted them with a mix of red, black, and green stains to make them appear older. The walls were redone with diamond plaster in a creamy color with a little sheen to it. Over the years, the original one-room house was expanded around a courtyard, now used as an outdoor living room, to eight hundred square feet, encompassing a living room, kitchen, bedroom, and bathroom.

A number of custom details make the guesthouse unique. The china cabinet is built in, with doors made of antique woodwork, and the bedroom and bathroom doors incorporate nineteenth-century wooden panels. Gold-leafed vintage tiles were fashioned into window valences. Lacy, who frequently uses the guesthouse for entertaining, made the kitchen a wonder in small-space efficiency by hiding the major appliances behind pale antique-white cabinetry. "I love to cook, and I can make a meal for twenty in that little kitchen!" Lacy declares. "I really enjoy entertaining in the outdoor living room." Lacy's place in the sun welcomes family and friends with historic atmosphere and a collection of treasures she is thrilled to share.

OPPOSITE:

ABOVE LEFT: Just beyond the entrance, the painted Italian chest sets the subdued color scheme for the guesthouse.

ABOVE RIGHT: Elaborate reproduction silver candlesticks flank a Peruvian painting of the Virgin and child. The little gilt-wood electrified lamps are French.

BELOW RIGHT: The tiny kitchen is actually very well equipped and even includes a washer and dryer. Lacy often uses it when entertaining in the courtyard. She had the brick floors stained red, black, and green in an effort to make them appear original to the house.

BELOW LEFT: This chest was reconstructed from pieces. On the right is a nineteenth-century gold cross. The pair of English paintings on wood were a gift from a friend.

ACKNOWLEDGMENTS

FOREMOST, I'D LIKE TO EXPRESS MY GRATITUDE to the formidable Harry Greiner, who is due credit for conceiving this book and who has been a dedicated partner throughout.

A great big thank-you to the team: Aliza Fogelson, editor; Alejandro Saralegui, writer; and David Chickey, book designer, for their skilled and keen collaboration in making all the components of this book coalesce into a body of work of which I am very proud.

I am indebted to Paige Rense, John Loring, Lisa Newsom, and Chuck Ross, for their enormous influence and nurturing early in my career.

A special thank-you to Roland Lee, for his enduring friendship and support.

My heartfelt thanks to colleagues, friends, and homeowners who contributed to this book in an invaluable way:

Barbara and Gary Aimes
David Arment and Jim Rimelspach
Carol Anthony
Kimberlie and Barclay Bloodworth
Edward (Barney) Brown
Marcia Brown
Marie Carty
Dianne Cash
Bunny and Omer Claiborne
Cece Cord
Mary Emmerling and Reg Jackson
John Fincher
Natalie Fitzgerald
Eugene Frank, M.D.
Alvin Friedman-Kien, M.D., and Ryo Toyonaga

Carol and Mark Glasser

John Gough

Peter Hallack

Sallie Ann and Bob Hart

Kim and Michael Haskell

Eddie Holler and Sam Saunders

Linda Mason Hunter

Martha Hyder

Mary and Chuck Kehoe

Kelly Klein

Nancy and Jack Lacy

Pearl Lau

Ann Lawrence

Ruth Hirshey Lincoln

Gloria List

Nedra Matteucci

Jeannette Meier

Caroline Monaco and Michael Halsey

Whitney Moore

Kristine de Navasquez

Ed North

Kerry Olson

Pam and Jesse Pierce

Paula Andros Provet and John A. Provet, M.D.

Steven Rockmore

Loree Rodkin

Ford Ruthling and Robert Mason

MaryJane and Frank Ryburn

John F. Saladino

Brian Saltzman, M.D.

Jane Smith

Carol Taylor

Adrienne and Gigi Vittadini

Linda Waterman

Gregg Yale

Last, I hold a special place of honor for my mentor, the late Arthur Smith, who guided me down my path long ago.

An early-nineteenth-century gem-studded French saint's crown from the collection of Harry Greiner and Peter Vitale sits atop eighteenth-century vellum-covered books from Mexico.

INDEX

Note: *Italicized* page references indicate photograph pages.
Related text in photo captions.